Encourage Me Now

SANDRA L. BUNDY

DEDICATION

To Jesus first and foremost because He has given me the passion, ability, and words with which to share His love with others.

Also to my husband Andrew for his love, encouragement, and support.

CONTENTS

SANDRA L. BUNDY

ACKNOWLEDGMENTS

I would like to thank my editor Florita H. Bundy along with Senior Editor Andrew C. Bundy for all of their hard work in preparing *Encourage Me Now* for publishing. Cover photo credit is given to Andrew C. Bundy for the beautiful snow path picture he took at Bryce Canyon National Park.

CHAPTER 1

THE NEED FOR ENCOURAGEMENT

The name of the Lord is a strong tower: the righteous runneth into it, and is safe.
Proverbs 18:10

"Lord Jesus, please encourage me now!" This has been my daily prayer as I seek to find encouragement for my soul. Knowing that Jesus is the giver of true encouragement, I seek Him to send it to me. As I stroll to the mailbox across my street, I ask Jesus to encourage me through my mail. Sometimes my prayers are answered at that moment; other times, I must wait on the Lord.

Helping or giving to others is a great way to lift up and encourage them. As I do my devotions of Bible reading, study, and prayer, God will lay on my heart someone I need to call, write, or give to. As I do this, my soul is encouraged. As Acts 20:35 reminds us, *"It is more blessed to give than to receive."* Luke 6:38 tells us that we cannot out give God. *"Give, and it shall be given unto you: good measure, pressed down, and shaken together, and running over, shall men give into your bosom. For with the same measure that ye mete withal it shall be measured to you again."*

As I pour my heart into writing this book, it is my passion and desire to be a support and mentor to anyone who seeks inspiration. God has given me the gifts of giving and encouragement. He has also put a passion in my heart to share this with others.

Pulling down the mailbox lid, I peek inside hoping that someone considered me important enough to take time to send a letter or card to. I see an envelope with my name on it. My heart jumps for joy. I tear into it

1

and pull out a card. It was sent from a lady to tell me how much she appreciates me as a friend. I know how much time and effort it takes to sit down and hand write a letter or card, so I feel very special. Taking the time to address and stamp an envelope is enough of a task to discourage many from writing to others. This means so much to me because this person is giving of herself and her time to me.

What encourages me most is when I write a card or give a gift to someone and they say "thank you." I love to give to others and encourage them. This is so natural for me because it is how God made me. Not wanting or expecting anything in return is the definition of true giving, but a "thank you" is like energy to my soul and heart to give more and more.

Thankfulness is evidence of contentment. I gave small gifts to children I was teaching once by pulling their names randomly out of a box. The more you attended Bible School, the more opportunity you had for your name being called at the end of the week for a prize. Some complained they only received one prize. I asked the group, "How many of you expected anything when you came tonight?" None of them raised their hands. I taught them to be content and thankful when they receive anything. I also taught them they should say "thank you" for receiving all of those treasures. I also made sure every child present received at least one gift just for coming to the church event.

Children need to be taught to say "thank you" and to be happy and content with what they have. Constantly wanting what others have leads to covetousness and discontentment in life no matter how blessed you are. If you have shelter, clothes, food, and family, you are so blessed by God. It seems in America, many think that if they do not have the latest phone, laptop, or gaming system with games, they are poor. The truth is that we Americans are so blessed that we take much for granted and think we deserve more. We need to stop trying to be like those around us that have so many materialistic items. Joy and contentment does not come from owning things, it comes from giving and doing for others. Feeling depressed? Stop thinking about yourself and start thinking about how you can help someone in some way. The return on helping and encouraging others far exceeds the amount of energy put into it. Christians cannot out give God, no matter how much they try.

The purpose I have set forth in writing this book is to encourage and to be a mentor, teaching others to encourage and be thankful. I give all glory and praise to my Savior, Jesus Christ, from this adventure and where it leads. My heart's desire is for my life to be used mightily to honor and lift up His name.

I therefore, the prisoner of the Lord, beseech you that ye walk worthy of the vocation wherewith ye are called, with all lowliness and meekness, with longsuffering, forbearing one another in love; endeavouring to keep the unity of the Spirit in the bond of peace.
Ephesians 4:1-3

CHAPTER 2

DREAM BIG

I press toward the mark for the prize of the high calling of God in Christ Jesus.
Philippians 3:14

"Go forth." As I decided to write this book, I had opportunities to talk to many people about it. I also have asked them to pray for me as I was seeking God about a decision to follow a dream. Some responded saying they thought it was too big of a dream. Already knowing what a mountainous endeavor it would be, I would reply, "It is a big dream. For it to happen, I know it would have to be all God and not me. His will be done. Thanks for your prayers. If you are going to dream, you might as well dream BIG!!!"

As I strolled on my walk one morning, the task ahead seemed too general, too broad, so I asked the Holy Spirit inside of me to help me with the words. I thought, "Not the whole book, only chapter one; not even chapter one, just the first few words." I once again sought the Holy Spirit for words and immediately they came, "Go forth." Those two words are my mission statement for my ministry. My goal is to go forth and to tell everyone about Jesus Christ and how He is the answer to any problem or hardship one will face.

My ministry verse is 1 Kings 19:11-12 "*Go Forth, and stand upon the mount before the LORD. And, behold, the LORD passed by, and a great and strong wind rent the mountains, and brake in pieces the rocks before the LORD; but the LORD was not in the wind: and after the wind an earthquake; but the LORD was not in the earthquake: And after the earthquake a fire; but the LORD was not in the fire: and*

4

after the fire a still small voice." As God encouraged Elijah with a still, small voice, may I also go forth and be a witness for the name of Jesus and an encouragement to all I will meet. Like Elijah, we feel as though we are the only ones out there who care about the things of God. When we open our eyes and our hearts and look around us, there are millions of Christians around the world who have Jesus Christ as their Savior and seek His glory. Also, there are so many people who are hurting and seeking an answer to fill their emptiness.

We will experience hardships in order for God to work through us to be a help to others later. It also molds our character and behavior to be more Christ like. My youngest son put up a Facebook status that made me cry and be proud of him all at the same time. I was running errands and was sitting at the bank waiting for my turn. I retrieved my phone from my purse and began scrolling on the Facebook newsfeed. I came across Caleb's status and began to read it. Then, it was my turn at the bank. I put my phone momentarily away and finished my banking business. I went back to my car and sat there and finished reading his status. He wrote, "I saw this video today (To This Day Project by Shane Koyczan on YouTube) (1. Koyczan) and I cried my eyes out....I was one of those kids. I was the fat kid that got picked on every day at school....I didn't know why they did it, it wasn't like I didn't know I was fat, it's not like I didn't see it every time I looked in the mirror. I wasn't ever mean to them, I didn't start anything. They just did it for the (fun) of it....I had to be taken out of my old school and put into home school because of how much I was getting picked on. Seeing this video today made me cry from thinking about how I was the fat kid that was bullied every day...and how today I made it past the bullies and all the names. On the outside, I made it look like the names didn't hurt...but they did...every last one of them felt like knives to my heart...but I made it past it and today I don't care how people think I look. When I look in the mirror.... I don't see pain, regret, doubt, ugly, anger, sadness, or pity anymore.....I simply see me." As I read his words, my eyes teared up and I felt so helpless because I didn't know the extent of his being bullied. My heart ached and I wanted to feel guilty as his mom. God keeps reminding me how that experience has shaped his life to be a sensitive, caring person to others who are experiencing the same things he went through and I should not feel guilty but excited to see the hand of God work miraculously in his life.

On his Facebook page, I posted, "Caleb, I am so proud of how much you have learned from that hard time in your life. I also remember how protective you were of others who were also being bullied. I know how bad the names hurt too. I was bullied because I could not speak well. It is amazing that now I enjoy being in front of people and speaking, especially when I am lifting up the name of Jesus, the true healer of any and all hurts.

Only He can fill that empty hole inside each of us. Now, it is your turn to be a help to anyone out there that is going through what you did because you understand completely. I love you to Mars and back. Love, Mom."

Many others posted to encourage him. Others posted "proud of you" comments. Some expressed how he is growing into a Godly young man. Then, his Uncle Jason who was able to use empathy because he had experienced the same exact circumstances wrote, "Caaaaaaaleeeeeeeb Buuuuuuundyyyyyyyyyy!!!!! (Think the famous boxing/wrestling announcer Michael Buffer!!!) I feel your pain....was called tub of lard...etc. when I was 10-12....but God IS faithful and I grew five inches and got skinny ...seriously though....kids are cruel so make sure to teach yours NOT to be that way!! You are growing into a fine and Godly young man....never forget the grace and mercy God has shown you so that you can show it to others."

His uncle was able to express empathy with Caleb because he had experienced the same exact bullying in the same way. I had been bullied and understood that concept; but I had never been called "fat" and could not understand that like his uncle could. We will all face trials in our lives; it is so important that we take those trials and turn them into ways to give God glory and to be a help and encouragement to others.

Look over your life and write down the trials you have experienced and then find ways of using those hard times to help others. Many people feel all alone like Elijah and think they are the only ones who have gone through the trial they are experiencing at that moment. We should be on the lookout for ways to encourage those who are hurting like we have hurt. Empathy is knowing exactly how an experience feels because you have gone through the same thing. Dream big and find ways to give God treasure through your tragedies.

When God puts a burden on one's heart to go and do a calling that is overwhelmingly frightening, he should first decide that even if the worst possible event occurs, that as long as he is in God's will, that all is well and will bring God glory. The worries and problems that we are most fearful of often do not come to pass. As a child, I was fearful of many things. First, I was fearful of monsters in the dark. This is a justified fear because the evil people who wish to do harm usually do so in the dark. For all of my life's years now, I have not had to even face a monster in the dark that tried to hurt me. Secondly, I was fearful of alligators. When I was a child, my church was across the street from a lake filled with alligators. I would have nightmares about alligators coming out of that lake and walking the miles to my house and coming into my bedroom to attack and eat me. In reality, I have always been extra careful around alligators and have not been attacked by one yet. This year at Vacation Bible School at my church, I actually held a two-foot gator in my arms and had my picture taken with it. I was able to check that off of my bucket list. Thirdly, I feared being kidnapped. I pray daily for God's hedge of protection. Psalms 91 is very precious and dear to me. God has put His hedge of protection around me and kept me safe. Worrying about possible happenings is a waste of time because most of the time it does not happen.

We are told to pray without ceasing. Praying instead of worrying will not give you ulcers or stunt your spiritual growth. One is not fully trusting when he is worrying. Commit every part of yourself, everyone, and everything you love to God as His. If someone or something is taken away, you are mentally and spiritually prepared to deal with it because you have willingly given it back to God already. If one has something that would hurt him to a point of being broken down and unable to cope ever again, then he has placed too much affection on that person or item. One should be able to lose everything and everyone in his life and still go forward for Jesus. This is only able to be done through surrendering all to Christ.

There have been many missionaries who have gone to the mission field and lost their lives or the lives of their loved ones. A Godly testimony and love for Jesus shines forth as they trust God even when tragedy hits hard. It is God's desire to have the tragedies we face become blessings. It is up to us to look for the blessings in our tragedies and learn to grow in them to be more Christ like.

Go forth and dream big is God's desire for each of His children. He calls out to each of us to be the best we can be for Him and His glory. It is important that we do not allow fear or worry to keep us from being completely in the will of God. Sometimes people are in God's will, but refuse to dream big because the cost is too much. They are happy in their comfort zone and do not want to trust God to work mightily in their lives. If every Christian was willing to stand up and dream big, we would have another Great Awakening and revival around the world where everyone would truly see the power of God.

Wherefore take unto you the whole armour of God, that ye may be able to withstand in the evil day, and having done all, to stand. Stand therefore. Ephesians 6:13-14a

CHAPTER 3

TRIUMPHANT OVER TRAGEDY

Behold, how good and how pleasant it is for brethren to dwell together in unity!
Psalm 133:1

The date April 15 has been memorable to me for many years now because it is the date that my daddy died in 1979. On Monday, April 15, 2013, another tragedy happened to America. As I watched ABC and NBC news, (2. ABC News.com) (3. The History Channel Website) (4. NBC News.com) many sad facts were revealed over the next few days. The 117th Boston Marathon was bombed by terrorists when all the families and friends were gathering around to watch their loved ones finish this amazing race. Two bombs exploded and two were found before they exploded. Three people were murdered by the bombs these terrorists planted including a Chinese national female graduate student at Boston University, a 29-year old female restaurant manager who went with her friend to take a picture at the finish line, and an 8-year old boy who was watching the race with his family. The boy's mom had to undergo brain surgery and his 6-year old sister lost a leg. Over 175 people were injured with eight being children. Some of the injured lost their limbs.

My heart is so heavy and frustrated that America is being attacked in such a cowardly way. My sadness turned into triumph when I saw my son's Facebook cover photo. Jacob, like many others, is a diehard Boston Red Sox fan. The picture showed the New York baseball emblem in blue and the Boston Red Sox emblem in red and in between, the words UNITED WE STAND.

The only thing that would unite the diehard New York Yankee and Boston Red Sox baseball fans during baseball season is empathy of experiencing terrorist bombings. Terrorists are trying to tear Americans apart, but what they are doing is bonding them together. Experiencing tragedy together is one of the fastest ways people connect and bond deeply. What makes America so strong as a nation is that from our very beginning we have fought hard for our freedom and rights. May God truly bless America and help her to continue to be the mighty, Godly nation she is. God bless America, please.

For five long, exhausting, frightening days, police and FBI were searching for the terrorists. During this time, a police officer had a shootout with the two brothers who left the bombs at the marathon route. Sadly, the police officer died along with the older brother. The younger brother terrorist ran away and hid. Boston citizens were asked to stay home and not go anywhere while the FBI and policemen looked for the terrorist.

A citizen went outside into his back yard and noticed blood on his boat cover. When he looked inside the boat and saw someone, he called the police. A swarm of agents and police officers rapidly arrived on the scene where there was at a standoff for about two hours. My husband and I watched the news anxiously waiting to see what would happen. Finally, the younger brother who was bleeding decided to give himself up. America breathed a sigh of relief as it all came to an end. Police, FBI, city, and state leaders were absolutely exhausted as they gave their media update to America stating that the whole ordeal had finally ended. My husband and I along with all of America were able to sleep well knowing it had ended.

As the national anthem was being sung at a Boston hockey game, thousands of patriotic, bonded Americans sang from the depths of their hearts to show that America is strong and we take care of our own and those who attack any of us. Since the beginnings of this courageous, independent country, we have had to depend upon each other. This attack was another incident where we jumped on the American eagle and rode it until the end. We have become accustomed to seeing our soldiers coming home without a leg or arm as they fight tirelessly to protect our citizens. We will never become accustomed to seeing men, women, and children killed or bloodily maimed in our homeland. May all of the generations of Americans learn to bond together and be the Christian nation that we began as so many years ago.

A personal tragedy to me was when my mother at 53 years of age experienced a brain aneurysm. A blood vessel in her brain ballooned and weakened so much that it exploded and started bleeding out. She was in her home early in the morning getting ready for work. My sister, Shelia, lived in another city but happened to be visiting my mom that weekend. My mom walked into the bedroom where my sister was sleeping and woke her up and said, "I feel funny" as she fell onto the bed where my sister was laying. A phone call was placed to 911 and an ambulance came and took my mom to the hospital. She had brain surgery and the aneurysm was clamped. The sight of tubes and devices all over my mom's body was quite unsettling.

My sister and I had already lost our daddy on Easter morning, 1979; so the thought of not having our mom or dad with us was a lot to bear. It was Easter morning and my sister and I went to the sunrise service at our church located across the street from Newnan's Lake. My dad had been sick with cancer for two years now and was bedridden because it had spread to his brain. A week earlier, I had gone into his room and put my arm around his head and just laid there holding my daddy. I was twelve so I understood he would be dying soon. I was crying, so my mom whispered to me not to let my dad see me crying. He could not do anything for himself at this point except move his blue grey eyes some. I grieved for the upcoming loss of my daddy before he even died. Then, I went out to play with my good friends. Playing made my chaotic life normal. I loved to ride bikes, climb trees, and make forts. I was able to escape the upcoming appointment with death that my family faced when I was outside playing.

That Easter morning, my sister and I sat on a blanket after the church service eating doughnuts and watching the sun rise into the sky. A woman came up to us and told us that our mother had called and we needed to go home immediately. Driving home, my sister and I did not talk; we knew what had happened and silently took in the idea of being fatherless. When we arrived home, our mom told us that our daddy had died. From that day forward, I claimed my Heavenly Father, God, as my earthly father too. In my mind, I was extra special to Him because I was fatherless. I knew He took special care of the widow, fatherless, and poor. Our family now met all three of these categories. Throughout the rest of my life, my faith would be increased tremendously due to my daddy's death. I would have preferred not to have lost my daddy; but I am so thankful and blessed that I did because of who I have become due to this hardship in my life.

As I looked at my mom in the ICU bed with tubes everywhere, I knew my life was about to once again change forever. My mom loved babies and was hoping so much to be a grandmother. My husband and I had been married for four years and did not have any children yet. My husband had cancer about three years after we were married which happened to be just a year before my mom's stroke. His doctor did surgery immediately and told us we had one month to try to have a baby before he would have to start radiation treatments. We would have to wait at least a year after his treatments were finished to try for children again. Due to my extremely painful endometriosis and my husband's cancer surgery, our chances of becoming pregnant were significantly lowered. I was so glad my mom was here to be an encouragement to us during this time before her stroke. My heart saddened as I knew she would not be able to babysit and help with the care of her grandchildren due to the effects of the stroke.

My sister became my mom's advocate and angel. She gave up her Accounting CPA job in order to take care of mom. She helped to motivate, heal, and rehabilitate my mom. Mom lived with my sister and her family for eleven years. Mom was able to be around my sister's children while they were growing up. Mom now lives with my Aunt Nancy (Mom's sister-in-law) and her family. My sister, my aunt, and both of their families have been such a blessing in taking care of mom.

It is such a blessing to see how God's goodness comes from tragedy. Now when something tragic happens, I start looking around for the blessings that God will be soon sending us. Tragedy teaches gratitude. I am so thankful for my family, my husband and sons, and everything we are blessed with. I am learning not to take anyone or anything for granted.

When tragedy hits your family, you sometimes wonder why. God knows the whole picture of our lives from beginning to end, and I know He has my best interest in mind. Jeremiah 29:11 is a verse that always encourages me when I am uncertain about why something is happening.

For I know the thoughts that I think toward you, saith the Lord, thoughts of peace, and not of evil, to give you an expected end. Jeremiah 29:11

CHAPTER 4

WHAT CHRISTIANS FEAR THE MOST –
TALKING WITH OTHERS ABOUT JESUS

And he said unto them, Go ye into all the world, and preach the gospel to every creature.
Mark 16:15

My oldest son, Jacob, graduated from the University of Central Florida with a Bachelor's degree in Business Administration Economics in August, 2013. He began Pastoral Studies at West Coast Baptist College, Lancaster, California in September of the same year. Since he was 12-years old, he knew that he was called into full-time ministry for God. He soon developed a passion for apologetics which is the logical defense of the truth of Christianity.

Jacob was able to attend a Josh McDowell apologetics seminar. He was a volunteer youth leader at a small church in Orlando, FL and was able to take some of the youth with him. He had decided that at the end of the seminar he would buy a certain book by Josh McDowell. Before he had a chance to do so, something amazing happened. This is the account in his own words:

So the craziest thing happened tonight at Josh McDowell's Jesus: "Fact or Fiction" seminar. I was able to go with three of the guys from my youth group and my roommate. By the time we got there and were trying to find a seat in the balcony (because the main floor of the auditorium was already full), the balcony had already filled up. So we went to a building (called the Epicenter) near the back of the church campus where the event was being held and watched it live on a projection screen. We sat with two other friends.

The seminar was incredible! I learned some very helpful new material to use in sharing my faith and perhaps the most amazing thing to me personally was when he discussed a recent archaeological breakthrough in Central Egypt he had been able to experience firsthand. They found a boatload of ancient copies of all kinds of manuscripts including several portions of books in the New Testament (i.e. Romans, 1 Corinthians, Mark, etc.) dating to earlier than A.D. 125! They also found a portion of the New Testament dating to 50 years of the original! If you know anything about ancient Biblical manuscripts and scholarly work on them, these are incredible breakthroughs!

Anyway, during the seminar they had us fill out these cards with information to be part of a drawing for books at the end. After McDowell had finished, he called off the first name and it was some adolescent to which McDowell gave a book he wrote specifically for adolescents. It was at this point that I leaned over to my friend, who was sitting beside me, and said, "If he calls my name, I'm jumping the row in front of me." No sooner than the words had escaped out of my mouth, Josh McDowell read aloud the words: "Jacob Bundy". My facial expression went from a smile (because I was kidding with my friend) to shock, and in a split second I jumped the row of chairs in front of me, bolted through the crowd in the epicenter and out the doors. I sprinted all the way down the sidewalk across the church campus and to the main auditorium, where I ran in the building, through the atrium, and into the lower deck of the main auditorium. I ran halfway up the aisle and shouted, "Mr. McDowell!" And for a split second there was this awkward aroma that filled the room where you could tell everyone in the room, including Mr. McDowell, was like, "Who is this kid?" I continued speaking after taking a deep breath because I was panting from the sprint over. "I'm Jacob Bundy. I was in the Epicenter!" The entire auditorium started laughing and applauding as I approached the stage. Mr. McDowell (who had already given away the book he was going to give me in the time it took me to sprint from the Epicenter to the auditorium) handed me the next book he had (which was the one I had said earlier that night I was going to buy!) and gave me a high-five. It made my night. God is good. What are the odds?"

When one has his heart's desire to serve God and tell others about Jesus, God will provide that person with the boldness and words to say. I am constantly praying to the Holy Spirit within me to give me boldness to talk to others and to give me the right words to reach them for Jesus. I also want to constantly learn more about God and the Bible so I can logically defend the truth of Jesus Christ and Christianity.

Jacob was able to go to another apologetics conference in Palm Beach, FL with a group from his University of Central Florida Baptist Collegiate Ministries. He even had his picture taken with Lee Strobel. He quoted Mr. Strobel on his Facebook page. "If Jesus Christ himself were to appear to you tonight, and He told you that He would grant you every prayer you made last week, would there be anyone new in the Kingdom of God?" – (Lee Strobel.)

This quote makes you think. It also makes you realize that prayer is important before we start to tell others about Jesus. We should pray every morning for God to give us opportunities, boldness, words, and knowledge to communicate the truth to others. We should also be praying for specific people to accept Jesus as their Savior. God will lay certain people strongly on your heart and you should pray for them and tell them about Jesus. Even if you don't know what to say, you already know your own salvation testimony and how Jesus works in your life personally.

Telling others about Jesus is what many Christians fear most. I think some would prefer to die for their beliefs before they would have to talk about them. The devil often uses this fear to his advantage. Even those who are considered the boldest Christians have times of extreme fear. Each Christian must seek the Holy Spirit inside of him to provide boldness to be brave and to talk to those who are not saved.

The wicked flee when no man pursueth: but the righteous are bold as a lion. Proverbs 28:1

CHAPTER 5

SIGNS OF A GREAT LEADER

For Thou art my rock and my fortress; therefore for Thy name's sake lead me and guide me. Psalm 31:3

There are many men and women who are mediocre as leaders. What is it that sets an individual apart as a really great leader? First, he must be willing to sacrifice his time, effort, and perhaps even money to attain to being the best. Second, he must be willing to be a help to those he leads and also not be afraid to get his hands dirty with the grunt work when needed. Finally, he must prepare himself spiritually so he may give to others and be an encouragement to them.

The first sign of a great leader is being willing to sacrifice and go above and beyond what is expected to make an impact on others. There are many leaders who lead without sacrifice. They put in what is asked of them, but never do more. As a teacher, my motto is to "go above and beyond". Students often actually sit down and figure out the least amount of effort just to pass a course or test. Instead, they should be doing their best to go above what is asked of them. If there was extra credit work offered in one of our sons' classes, we would encourage them to always do it.

One who is a great athlete doesn't necessarily mean that he or she is a great leader on the team. The really great athletes are the ones who put forth extra sacrifice. Many athletes are naturally gifted, but to be the best, extra effort is mandatory. The captains of the football teams are usually not just great players, but they have a passion for the game and share it with the team. Excitement and passion spread like wildfire. We need more passionate leaders who share their excitement with others. We need more visionaries who are not afraid of risking failure for great success. Becoming comfortable in our "boxes" does not allow for greatness.

Secondly, a great leader is helpful to those he leads. I am reminded of our first United States president, General George Washington. John Maxwell, in his book, The Five Levels of Leadership, (5. Maxwell) tells the story of how great leaders are willing to get their hands dirty with grunt work:

One day during the American Revolutionary War, George Washington rode up to a group of soldiers trying to raise a beam to a high position. The corporal who was overseeing the work kept shouting words of encouragement, but they couldn't manage to do it. After watching their lack of success, Washington asked the corporal why he didn't join in and help. The corporal replied quickly, "Do you realize that I am the corporal?" Washington very politely replied, "I beg your pardon, Mr. Corporal, I did." Washington dismounted his horse and went to work with the soldiers until the beam was put into place. Wiping the perspiration from his face, he said, "If you should need help again, call on Washington, Your Commander In Chief, and I will come."

When a superior is seen being willing to be a help amongst his people, he becomes a great leader to them. Too many prideful men and women refuse to lower themselves to the positions of those they lead. This actually lessens the level of leadership in the minds of the people.

Lastly, a great leader prepares spiritually each morning and fills himself up with the Word of God and prayer so he is able to give back to all those who will need him throughout the day. If a leader goes out into his day empty, his leadership will also portray emptiness. It is imperative that he has had personal growth in his relationship with Jesus in the morning so as to be able to allow what he has learned each day to flow off him and onto everyone he meets and leads. It is important that the great leader does not become prideful and want glory for his great or significant accomplishments. As our Holy Spirit always reflects the glory back on Jesus, we also should be a reflector of all our accomplishments to Jesus.

Our world needs great leaders. We need leaders who are not seeking to be served or have everything given to them. Many young men and women today expect people to give to them and they feel that they deserve everything their parents have worked 30-40 years to get or accomplish. We need great leaders who are willing to sacrifice, work hard, and be willing to assist those they lead. We need leaders who spiritually prepare themselves in the mornings strengthening their personal relationship with their Savior, Jesus Christ. After all, He is the Greatest Leader of all.

Lead me in Thy truth, and teach me; for Thou art the God of my salvation; on Thee do I wait all the day. Psalm 25:5

CHAPTER 6

ONLY ONE YOU – INDIVIDUALITY

Before I formed thee in the belly I knew thee; and before thou camest forth out of the womb I sanctified thee, and I ordained thee a prophet unto the nations. Jeremiah 1:5

Each person has fingerprints that are unique from everyone else in the whole world. God, your Creator, chose every detail about you. He decided the color your hair, eyes, and skin would be. He made a DNA blueprint that determined how tall you would be, what body type you would have, and even what personality you would possess.

Some people tear themselves down so easily and often with negative words about their self-image. We think we are being humble and righteous. Actually, we are telling the Creator of all things how horrible, fat, ugly, and disgusting His artwork is.

We need to focus on the "here and now" of how we look; accept it, thank God for it, and be content at this very moment with who we are. We cannot improve ourselves in any way effectively until we accept ourselves first and foremost. When we have come to the conclusion to accept it and ask God to help us make plans and goals to be the best Godly men and women we can be, then we are truly ready to make life changing choices for His glory and not our own.

Every man and woman wants to improve in some way; whether it is losing a few pounds, eating healthier, using sunscreen, reading for self-improvement, or spending more time with loved ones and friends. The first step to being your best is making achievable, encouraging goals. When we reach a goal, we then need to make another goal until we are finally where we feel God wants us to be.

God made people with different body shapes, minds, personalities, and talents. A goal that is right for one person may not be right for another. Seeking God's face and asking Him to give individualized goals is the place to begin. Areas to set goals are physical, mental, emotional, and spiritual. It is important to pray and even fast as you seek God's leading for your life.

Physical goals could be to eat fish three times a week, fruits and vegetables three times a day, and to walk for 45 minutes five days a week. Your goals need to be specific and achievable. The real goal in your mind is that you want to lose weight and be healthy. Often your mind gets fixated on the number on the scale to the point of depression, so you decide to weigh only one time a week.

Mental goals could be to read daily, to play mind improvement games on your phone one time a week, and to memorize a new word and its meaning and a Bible verse weekly. The mental goals would be person specific depending on his or her passions and desires. I enjoy reading encouraging books that help me in my life at that moment in time. For example, books about being a wife, rearing teen boys, teaching, etc. I gain support and energy in knowing the stories of how others have lived through the same types of experiences I am living now. I also get great ideas on new ways to accomplish my goals in life. Some ideas work wondrously and some are utter failures.

Emotional goals could be to spend "alone time" with each family member once a week, to take time for yourself to do something just for you (this is actually a benefit to the whole family because you are able to relax and get rid of stress), or to seek to be joyful and content no matter what is happening in your life.

Spiritual goals should be made according to where you are in your spiritual life. A new Christian should focus on consistency of Bible reading and learning from what they have read as opposed to reading through the Bible two times in a year. So many Christians are not consistent in their Bible reading because they have not made it a priority or habit. It takes approximately 40 days to make an action a habit. Consistency in daily Bible reading and prayer are great ways to grow spiritually as a Christian.

Spiritual goals for a new Christian could be to read one verse a day, think about it throughout the day, and apply it to his or her life. For example, Psalm 119:11 states, *"Thy Word have I hid in my heart that I might not sin against Thee."* One could pick this verse apart and really try to understand it and what it really means. "Thy Word" means the Bible. "Hid in my heart" is talking about memorizing God's Word. "That I might not sin against Thee" means that when I am tempted to sin, I can quote a verse to help me not to sin. You might decide to memorize a verse and James 4:7 is chosen. *"Submit yourselves therefore to God. Resist the devil, and he will flee from you*". This encourages you to learn about how Jesus resisted temptation. You read the verses about Jesus resisting the devil in the wilderness after fasting for 40 days and you learn from His example. This process can teach a new Christian how to deal effectively with temptation.

As a Christian grows, he may seek God's face in how he can set spiritual goals. Some spiritual goals could be to read God's Bible through once a year, to pray daily for specific people you want to pray for (family, sick people, missionaries, etc.), and to ask God daily how you may be an encouragement to someone in your life (get well card, note of encouragement, text to say hi, etc.). This, once again, should be sought through prayer and fasting. Fasting does not have to be food; it could be doing without something for a day to focus more on prayer and others. (Examples: Facebook, TV, sweets, games, a meal, etc.)

After you set goals for yourself, write them down and put it someplace where you will see them daily and then read them again and again to remind and encourage you. Some people like to put their goals as a note in their phone making them easily accessible. Being accountable to a friend is a great way to stay on task in achieving goals. If you feel you have set unrealistic goals; change them and make them achievable. Reaching a goal is an encouragement as opposed to never being able to reach it or it taking too long to reach it. Once you have reached a goal, set another goal to keep yourself growing as a person.

It is also important to review your goals annually to see if they need to be changed. Each January is a perfect time to review your old goals and to set new ones. As you are growing as a person, you may see that you are able to stretch yourself and your goals or keep some the same if they are working well for you. If you have a huge goal, you could also set weekly or monthly mini steps to the main goal. This is encouraging as you see your progress. One should have at least one goal for each category of physical, mental (academic or work), emotional (time with others and alone time), and spiritual. One may wish to have several goals for each category. Think, pray, and fast about what would work best for your life.

I press toward the mark for the prize of the high calling of God in Christ Jesus.
Philippians 3:14

CHAPTER 7

A PRISONER OF SELF-IMAGE

I will praise Thee; for I am fearfully and wonderfully made; marvelous are thy works; and that my soul knoweth right well. Psalm 139:14

Women pay attention to what other women wear, what color and style of hair they have, what kind of shoes, jewelry, makeup, and facial expression they show. To illustrate, I was attending a party once when a group of ladies arrived. Within seconds, I observed how much time was probably taken to get dressed, if they were in a good or bad mood, if they dressed up or down, if they came right from work, and how they felt about themselves at that very moment. Within about five minutes, an observation had been made that the first woman came directly from work, the second was very tired, the third felt overwhelmed, the fourth was happy, and the fifth was excited to be with adults. During this time, I was personally trying very hard to feel good about my self-image.

We have three sons attending college, so we are saving money to the best of our abilities with me not working outside our home. My two youngest sons are homeschooled seniors and are dual enrolled at the local community college. I still believe they need me as mom and home school teacher to guide them with study and organization skills. One big way I help with finances is by cutting my own hair; I also do not have my hair colored. Yes, I am an angelic brown-haired beauty with silver highlights. I actually love the freedom of not worrying about my hair color or the expense anymore.

A funny occurrence happened to me earlier in the day of the party. I decided to cut my hair a little shorter than I usually do. I have seen hair stylists put ladies' hair in a ponytail and cut just above the holder. I thought that I could do the same process with no glitches. So I lifted my hair over my head with my left hand and started cutting with shears in my right hand. This procedure took a little longer than I anticipated. As my right arm began to tire and the ponytail holder began to slip, my straight line became quite askew. I accomplished my goal leaving me with a hand full of hair attached to a pony tail holder.

Grabbing a mirror, I gawked at the back of my hair, and wanted to cry. I anticipated this chore to be effortless and pain free. I was tremendously mistaken. My heart sank to bleakness as I remembered my husband and I would be gathering with others for food and fellowship at a friend's home that night. I tried without success to correct the unevenness of my hair butchery. I decided to call and make an appointment for a haircut. I was in emotional pain when I paid $37 for my renovated hair style.

Women are examined wherever they venture. Each woman makes a decision every time she walks out her door concerning what she is wearing. Will she be embarrassed if anyone she knows sees her dressed how she is? She may have finished her walk or exercise routine for the day and be sweaty, but she has no time to shower before she must run to the grocery store. Of course she sees someone she knows, apologizes for her sweaty aroma, and explains why she is this way. Men could care less that others see them covered in dirt and grease at the auto parts store as they purchase the last part they need to finish the job of repairing the truck. They certainly are not going to get a shower before they run to the store.

Women are often prisoners of self-esteem. At an early age we are told how beautiful we are. This is beneficial because no matter how outwardly attractive we are to others, in the eyes of our parents, we are princesses. If mom and dad do not tell us we are beautiful, the psalmist David tells us how our Creator made us: Psalm 139:14 states, *"I will praise Thee; for I am fearfully and wonderfully made; marvelous are thy works; and that my soul knoweth right well."* The point is God created us and He sees us as His beautiful masterpiece and we have no right to disagree with the Creator of all.

All women can add great beauty to themselves with confidence and a smile. People will usually believe what your face is telling them. You may be overweight, heading toward fifty or beyond, and not as held together in some places like you used to be, but at the same time be very confident in who you are. A good self-motivating talk to encourage yourself is that no matter what size, age, or shape you are in, you can be your best at that moment in time. As God leads you to better yourself, you can become healthier. The thought here is to be happy and content now and thank God for who and what you are.

SANDRA L. BUNDY

Who can find a virtuous woman? for her price is far above rubies. Proverbs 31:10

CHAPTER 8

THE GIFT OF ENCOURAGEMENT

Wherefore comfort yourselves together, and edify one another, even as also ye do.
1 Thessalonians 5:11

One of the spiritual gifts from God is encouragement. If you have this gift, it is natural to be an up-lifter to those around you. There are many ways to help someone's day progress smoother. Three categories of ways we can encourage are personal touch, time, and gifts.

The first category is personal touch. One actually makes contact with the person by making a home visit, a phone call, or a text. This leads to a conversation. Most people like to tidy up their home before visitors come, so a phone call prior to the visit will be much appreciated. Face to face interaction is greatly appreciated by those who are elderly and are not able to leave the house very often. It is also much welcomed by those in nursing homes. Some people go for days without meaningful human touch.

A phone conversation shows the person they are worth your time and effort. Hearing someone's voice may be the only contact with the outside world one has all week. Some people do not like face to face conversation, but they are very skilled at phone "chitchat."

A phone conversation requires one's full attention, so in today's society, many would prefer a text message over a phone call. One may text a message, take a few minutes to load laundry or check on the children, and then send another text message. With texting, the personal touch of the voice is missing, but few complain about it.

My husband and I are the Sunday school teachers of the young adult singles class at our church, ages 18-28. Our class convinced us to get texting on our phones because texting is this age group's mainstay of communication. We could easily communicate with the whole class through one group text. Whether they are in a college class or at work, we could communicate with them at any time and they could respond when they were free to do so. Now, we use texting daily as a form of communication and encouragement to others.

One uses the personal touch method of visits, calls, and texting by giving words of praise, encouragement, and also a listening ear. There are times when someone just needs to say something and/or be heard. A positive word of praise lifts one's spirit mightily. One may be feeling like giving up and quitting, but your words of encouragement and gratefulness could be the small spark that is needed to light the fire once again. Never underestimate the power of positive, uplifting words.

Another way to encourage is to give our time to others. This may be accomplished in a variety of ways such as helping a family move, mowing a widow's yard, or driving someone to a doctor's appointment. By sitting and talking with someone and listening to him talk about his week, one is being an encouragement by the time you spend with him.

The third category of encouragement is by giving. God has given me the gift of giving. I love to look for items for people and give it to them as a gift of encouragement. It truly is more blessed to give than to receive. I listen to people to understand what their likes are and find gifts that I know they will enjoy. A gift does not have to be expensive. It just needs to be given in love and care. No matter how many gifts I give to others, I cannot out give God because I am doing it to glorify and uplift the name of Jesus.

Everyone has the ability to encourage. A smile or kind word is free to give and is golden to receive. The dollar store has many nice $1 items that would help to encourage anyone. A card or letter mailed to me is one of my favorite gifts to receive. It tells me that I am important enough to the person because they take the time and effort to write and send it to me. Everyone is capable of giving something; even if it is only a smile and a "hello" to those you meet.

Give, and it shall be given unto you; good measure, pressed down, and shaken together, and running over, shall men give into your bosom. For with the same measure that ye mete withal it shall be measured to you again. Luke 6:38

CHAPTER 9

JESUS PLEASERS, NOT PEOPLE PLEASERS

But if from thence thou shalt seek the LORD thy God, thou shalt find him, if thou seek him with all thy heart and with all thy soul. Deuteronomy 4:29

There will be times in your life when you have to make a decision. Do I please man or do I please Jesus? Go to God in prayer and ask Him to lead you in the right way to handle the situation. Sometimes, He will lead you to leave the problem in His hands and He takes care of all of it. I enjoy this type of circumstance because you do not have to do anything but trust in God to take care of it. It is so important that you do not run ahead of Him and try to make things happen. For some people, this is like asking them to hold back an ocean wave; for others, it is very peaceful. Seeing God's hand working in their lives increases their faith and trust in Him significantly.

Other times, He will lead you to do something or say something to deal with the situation yourself. Make sure you have taken time to seek His face in prayer and are not handling it in your own fleshly way. It is very natural to want to run ahead of God and take care of the problem. It is critical that you do not do this. God's ways of solving the problem are always better than anything our minds can conceive. At times, this will be very difficult. Your tendency may be to solve the problem or trial out on your own. Learn to trust in God and follow His leading. A trial or problem will be less stressful and often be much shorter if you allow God to teach you instead of bucking God's lead.

There will be situations when you will have to decide to stand up for something you believe in or just go along with the flow of the people around you. You may even feel like you are the only one standing for what you know in your heart is right. This can cost you something. Your "friends" may leave you out in the cold or even ostracize you. Your family may try to tell you that you are overreacting. When your loved ones, those who are closest to you tell you that you are overreacting or taking your belief too far, you may feel totally isolated and alone. This is the time to seek the Holy Spirit for comfort. As a Christian, we have the Holy Spirit with us to help us through every situation. We are promised in Hebrews 13:5 that we will never be alone. This is also a time of spiritual growth because you feel like no one agrees with you and no one is on your side. It teaches you that, no matter what, Jesus is there for you through whatever you are facing. Follow God's leading and He will bring about the right answer for what to do.

God's timing is not equal to our timing. We want our problems to be gone and to be gone now! God's ways can be slow. Waiting on the Lord to work in the hearts of people because He is longsuffering and patient can be exasperating. We want God's help, but we want it done our way. This seldom happens. Many times I will think in my mind of how the problem can be solved. Then as I watch God's hand at work in my life, I am always amazed at how small of a mind I have to comprehend His magnificence and how He works.

Wait on the LORD: be of good courage, and he shall strengthen thine heart: wait, I say, on the LORD. Psalm 27:14

CHAPTER 10

CONSISTENCY IS KEY

But seek ye first the kingdom of God, and his righteousness; and all these things shall be added unto you. Matthew 6:33

Over time, consistency is the key to doing something well. Many times, a person will create a monstrosity of a goal that overwhelms him within weeks. To avoid the anxiety that comes with keeping up with such a task, he decides to quit altogether. It is better to do something small and be consistent than to attempt something big and quit before any progress is made. In time, you will become accustomed to the small task set before you and adding to it is not stressful, but desired. As years pass and you slowly add to your task, it becomes a desired task that is now part of you that you enjoy and want to do.

Consistency in small steps can climb a mountain or run a marathon. One must train and build up to such great achievements. One cannot just wake up one morning and say, "I think I want to hike across the Grand Canyon." One must make a list of needed supplies, spend months honing skills, and prepare mentally for such a magnificent enterprise. The same mentality should be applied to all aspects of our lives. We want to see the decorated cake; but we don't want to collect and measure the ingredients, lay out our needed tools, and take the time to bake the cake.

When one makes a goal, he should list his short-term objective and long-term mission. One feels like he has achieved much when a small mark is met and motivated to continue on to his ultimate destination. As time passes, and he matures and changes, his ultimate destination may also change. He may even realize that his ultimate target will always be beyond him, but shooting for the stars is his ambition. A college student realizes that obtaining 100% on every task and test assigned is unachievable, but that is what he has his sights set on.

It is important to start teaching one's children consistency at an early age. A child looks to his parents as role models. He is more likely to do what you do than what you say. If you don't want your sons looking at women who are inappropriately dressed, start teaching them to turn their heads when they are toddlers. It will become an automatic habit when someone is dressed inappropriately for them to turn away. Matthew 5:28 says, *"But I say unto you, That whosoever looketh on a woman to lust after her hath committed adultery with her already in his heart."*

Parents are responsible for their child's learning of character. We teach best by our lifestyle. What you spend the most time and money on is what is important to you. My Heavenly Father is first priority to me. I show my family this by getting up before everyone and having a time of Bible reading, prayer, and spiritual growth through study. The Holy Spirit and I are best friends. He goes with me everywhere and sees everything I see. I want to start my morning off on the right foot spiritually by absorbing God's Word. It arms me against temptation and hard times that I will face during my day.

After God, my next priority is my husband. As my sons are nearing the time that they will be sprouting wings and flying off into manhood, I am realizing that I need to spend more time preparing myself for being alone with my husband again. As a mom, you have so many arms and voices pulling at you that sometimes your husband is forgotten as a priority. Babies must be fed, changed, and taken care of. School age children need help with homework and baked goodies for their school bake sales and activities. Teenagers still need mom, but less often. As mom, we will always be a part of our children's lives, but less and less as time goes by. Our husbands will always be a part of our lives until "death do us part."

Spouses should be consistently working together on their marriage. We invest in our most important relationship daily with either deposits or withdrawals. It takes effort to constantly be uplifting and encouraging to someone who is gruff, tired, and irritable. Work takes a toll on our husbands. They want to be welcomed home to their wife and children with happiness and excitement to see daddy. They also need alone time to unwind from the stresses of work. It would be wise not to ask anything of your husband until he has had thirty minutes to an hour to decompress. He may also be hungry and irritable from a low sugar level of not eating since lunch, so having dinner ready for him always makes him happy.

Love is expressed in staying with someone over the years through sickness, surgery, in-law problems, deaths of loved ones, loss of job, rearing your children together, building or buying a new home, choosing a car, and vacations. These are only a few challenges you will face over your lifetime. You may be wondering why I listed vacations. I have a funny and embarrassing story to tell.

My husband and I saved money in order to go to the Grand Canyon as a family. We flew together and visited many wonderful places like Bryce Canyon, Zion National Park, and the North and South rims of the Grand Canyon. While staying in an amazing cabin at the north rim, the whole family went on a long and strenuous hike down into the canyon. We finally arrived back at our cabin after hours of hiking.

My husband and I decided to do some laundry. We left our 16, 14, and 13 year old sons in the cabin to relax and rest. We drove a couple miles to the laundry facility and I stayed to start the laundry. My husband drove back to the cabin to check on the boys and to bring them to help fold the clothes. The scene he arrived to at the cabin is one he will never forget as long as he lives. There were three law enforcement Park Rangers standing at our cabin door with guns holstered questioning our sons. My youngest son had been agitating his two brothers by singing and refusing to stop. After trying countless ways to make him stop, he was finally locked outside the cabin. He was yelling so much that it caused the neighbors to call security reporting that they thought a woman was being beaten.

Our oldest son was being questioned by the rangers. He explained everything to his father who was embarrassed and frustrated with the whole childish event. He had our oldest son show his license proving his age. The boys were released to the care of their dad. My husband made our sons promise they would not tell me and ruin my vacation. I remember when they all arrived at the laundry facility with somber faces. I was able to live the rest of our vacation in blissful ignorance. What a wonderful husband to shield me at that time. Months later, we laughed together as I was finally told the shameful Bundy boys story. No matter what happens that embarrasses you to death, just keep on being consistent in loving and teaching your children character and God's Word.

But Jesus said, Suffer little children, and forbid them not, to come unto me: for of such is the kingdom of heaven. Matthew 19:14

CHAPTER 11

OPENING BLOSSOMS

I beseech you therefore, brethren, by the mercies of God, that ye present your bodies a living sacrifice, holy, acceptable unto God, which is your reasonable service. Romans 12:1

So much work is put into growing and producing a beautiful flower. It begins with a seed that must be watched and cared for. The right amount of light, sunshine, and water is absolutely critical to the success of this process. After much time and effort are put into the ongoing master plan, it may come as a surprise when the matured flower actually begins to bud.

The same is true of a new mother and baby. She begins with doing everything for the little one from feeding and burping to changing diapers. She carries him everywhere and does everything for him. Without his mother's help and care, he would surely die. As one becomes a mother, one has chosen to spend the next 18 years or longer thinking about others before herself. She must take into account how what she does or says will affect the children gathered at her feet.

There are times when God's divine intervention through your prayer is the only solution to a situation. You must wait upon the Lord and consistently seek Him in supplications for His will. Words are not able to change circumstances sometimes. Your first inclination is to jump in and make everything the way you think it should be, but you know that would be futile and would cause more damage than good. So, you patiently wait upon the Lord and earnestly seek His face. You cry out to Him in your heartache and sorrow knowing that the whole situation is in His hands and

He will take care of all of it in His perfect timing. Impatience makes you want to run out in the middle of the situation and flag down everyone involved because you see the train wreck coming. You cry tears and your knees become worn as you kneel before your Holy Father for comfort and reassurance.

You read and claim scripture verses for comfort. You scream to the Lord in your mind that you have been praying about this for years and that God should bless your faithfulness to Him in this matter. As moms, when we see our children going through something painful, our first response is to run to them and make the pain go away. This is not always healthy. Our children must experience pain in order to learn from it and know that they can survive even when it hurts. Pain makes us strong and helps us to know that we can bear the hard times. We learn that pain is not the end of the world. We begin to understand with wisdom that life goes on and the dark rain clouds eventually go away. God is so good to give us a reprieve when we look to Him.

A mistake that many of us make is to run back to our comfort zone. Our comfort zone may be a myriad of events. It may be the wrong person in a relationship, a job that eats away at our soul, or a friend that lead us down a path of destruction. We stay there even when we know it is not right or healthy for us. We want to get rid of the pain so much that we are willing to suffer a lifetime of misery to avoid a few weeks or months of pain. Wisdom seems to fly out the window when we face life's toughest battles.

How does one face the situations that seem to overcome and attack? He must go to God and seek His face earnestly in prayer. Soak yourself in His Word. Don't run back to the comfort zone to avoid the pain. Immediately throw out all of the objects that remind you of the comfort zone. Avoid going to places that remind you of the person, job, friend, etc. and replace the empty space with Godly, positive activities and thoughts. Listen to Godly, encouraging music to uplift you. Read through the Psalms which act as a salve to an open wound. Many of our problems do not even compare to King David's. Have someone keep you accountable to your decision. You will have weak and confusing times because of the pain. Seek friends who will brighten your day. Don't focus on the comfort zone by talking about it a lot. Talk about your decision and how you feel about the emptiness and sadness, then give it to God and fill those thoughts with God.

Distraction is an excellent way to keep your mind off of your problems. Start a new hobby, make new friendships, go to new places, and be around people. Do not isolate yourself as this may lead to you running to your comfort zone. God uses time to heal; this is such a true statement. Take it one day at a time. Seek to make yourself feel better by being a help and encouragement to others. True happiness comes from giving to others. I have heard the saying "This too shall pass" based on 2 Corinthians 4:17 and I hold fast to this wisdom. This phrase is talking about when we seem so overwhelmed that we think we are stuck in the situation forever. God tells us in Psalm 30:5 that the hard time will pass and glory and joy comes in the morning. Wait upon the Lord and watch His hand work in your life to do amazing works that we cannot even imagine.

As I think back over a specific personal situation in my life, I thank God for His help to protect, lead, and encourage as our family progressed past a time that we seemed to be stuck in, to a time that we are now all on firm ground and walking in the right direction. When something in your life is keeping you from following God's perfect will, you must be willing to give up that item or person. Knowing God's will and staying on His path is one of life's greatest blessings.

Pray without ceasing. 1 Thessalonians 5:17

CHAPTER 12

TIME: THE BEST GIFT OF ALL

Behold, how good and how pleasant it is for brethren to dwell together in unity!
Psalm 133:1

If a child is asked if he would rather have a toy or spend time playing a game with his dad; most of the time, he would choose time with dad. Toys come and go, but undivided time with a parent is priceless. As I look back to my childhood, I have a few memories that have stayed with me about my dad. He became sick with cancer when I was ten and died two years later. I remember when he took my younger brother and me to the local department store and bought us candy orange slices. I remember a certain day he took me fishing. He caught a stingray and I can still see that fish and feel the fear that came over me when I saw it. I would not go near it. I also remember when my dad was close to death and took his last trip to Georgia to say goodbye to his family. He looked so tired and sickly. His head was bald and he appeared about twenty years older than his true age of 58.

These memories are special because we were spending time together. My last memory of my dad is from a week before his death where I laid beside him, missing him already in my heart. I was so blessed to have a daddy who loved, cared for, and spent time with his children. Life is precious and should not be taken for granted. One does not know what the next day has in store.

It should be a goal of each parent to spend at least an hour a week with each child giving his or her undivided attention. This investment of time will pay off later with extremely high dividends. Each child will feel cared about and will be more open to talking to his parents. One should research what the child is interested in and seek to spend occasions with them in their passion. Some areas of passion may be books, movies, video games, sports, ballet, debate, cheerleading, track, etc. These passions may also change as they mature. One day your child may wish to be a garbage man and then the next day a lawyer. One should not bash a child's dreams, but encourage them to dream and dream big.

Our son, Jacob, just came and told me he received an A in his most difficult college class, Mathematic Economics. This was a recommended class as a prerequisite to the Master's Degree program. He was planning on getting his MBA, so he registered for this class. After starting the class, he was notified that the full-time MBA program had been shut down and only offered part-time and it would take three years before he could finish instead of the one year program that he had planned on. This turned out to be a closed door in his life, so he will now start Bible College for Pastoral Studies in the fall instead of pursuing a MBA degree. He did not have to take Mathematic Economics to graduate, only as a prerequisite to the MBA program. It turned out to be the most challenging class of his college career. He spent the first two weeks constantly with the teacher during office hours. He also said that this was the most mentally demanding and competitive class he had to face. He spent countless hours working on this class, including twenty hours studying for the final exam alone. He was determined to get an A, and he did. As a mom, I was constantly praying for and encouraging him. I know God used this class to show him that when he faces adversity in the future, he will again go to God in prayer with hard work to succeed.

Jacob has faced physical distress by playing Division 1 college football and now he has faced mental affliction with his hardest college class. God is preparing him for his future that will have difficult times that probably won't compare to these two hardships. These years at college have prepared him in a variety of ways for his future. He can always look back and say, "This is hard, but not as hard as playing Division 1 football or Math Econ class." As we struggle through the hard steps of life, if feels as though the tough times will never end. When we finally hit the finish line and look back at our trial, we see that the Holy Spirit was with us encouraging us the whole way. He truly is the Great Comforter who will never leave nor forsake us no matter what we are going through.

Let, I pray thee, thy merciful kindness be for my comfort, according to thy word unto thy servant. Psalm 119:76

CHAPTER 13

REJOICE EVERMORE

But let all those that put their trust in thee rejoice: let them ever shout for joy, because thou defendest them: let them also that love thy name be joyful in thee. For thou, LORD, wilt bless the righteous; with favour wilt thou compass him as with a shield. Psalm 5:11-12

Waking up this morning, Psalm 118:24 is plastered in my thoughts: *"This is the day which the Lord hath made, we will rejoice and be glad in it."* Deep inside I knew I would be facing something that would be difficult, but God was letting me know that He is in control no matter what and I need to always trust in Him and rest in His care. I started my day as usual with prayer and devotions.

A few hours later I received a phone call from my husband's doctor's office asking for him. I gave them his cell phone number and told them it would be alright to call him at work. Andy had gone to the lab the day before and had blood drawn. He does this occasionally as a precaution due to some medicines he has to take. I am a registered nurse so I knew the office doesn't usually call a patient back unless there is a reason. My first thought was to immediately call him at work and see what was happening. Then I realized I would probably keep the doctor's office from reaching him, so I decided to wait until he arrived home to talk with him about it.

When Andy arrived home, I asked him if the doctor's office had reached him and he said, "Yes." I proceeded to ask "why?" when he did not automatically tell me. A memory came back to me of another time he came home from work and told me on a Friday that he had a potentially cancerous tumor, and the doctor would perform surgery on Monday. He was so young at only 25 years of age to be facing such a surgery. I was 23 years old and at that time we did not have any children either. After surgery, we had about one month to try to have a baby before my husband started radiation treatments to fight the cancer cells inside of him. God did not give us a child at that time because he knew that in a year my mom would have an aneurysm burst in her brain and that would be too much for us to handle.

My thoughts return to the present when Andy tells me that the doctors' office said his liver enzymes are elevated and they would draw blood again in a month to monitor. The liver is the largest internal organ and God has given it many amazing jobs like filtering the blood and keeping the body clean by removing toxins, storing energy in the form of glycogen, helping with blood clotting, and producing bile to aid in digestion of fats. Needless to say, the liver is a very important, hard-working organ that assists the body in a variety of ways.

On went my prayer warrior helmet and I started praying for God to take care of the situation and His will to be done. We agreed not to tell anyone at this time until his blood is tested again in a month. Andy has been taking cholesterol medicine for years and it may have just been too much for his liver. He had radiation treatments in his abdominal region for his cancer that may have affected his internal organs and made them more susceptible. His medicine is half the dose where it would usually affect the liver.

It is futile to worry. I gave it to God and remembered the verse He gave me that very morning, allowing me to rest in His arms. I take my hands off of the situation and pray allowing God to work in our lives. That Wednesday night, our family visited our friends' church and he preached about how nothing is impossible with God. This was like a healing salve to an open sore. We both needed encouragement and God gave it to us. We enjoyed visiting with our friends. Little did they know how much they encouraged us that night.

The next day was October 31st. I woke up with another verse on my mind, Philippians 4:6, *"Be careful for nothing, but everything by prayer and supplication let your requests be made known unto God."* As I lay there in my bed thinking about how important it is to ask God about every little aspect of our lives, I decided to ask if it would be alright for me to go on my daily walk. I had peace that it was, so I dressed to head out.

As I am walking the same route I have taken for years, I am praying that no unclean spirit would prosper that Halloween day. As soon as I finish that thought, a black snake slithers across the sidewalk in front of me where my very next step would be. I stop and scream! I think I scared the snake more than it scared me. It hastily crawls into the woods and out of my sight. After my heart starts beating again, I back up and briskly walk far away from the woods to continue on my way.

My mind and body finally settles down about a quarter of a mile later when I am facing a man walking toward me on the sidewalk. I have been passing this man and his home for years praying for his whole family's salvation. When I first started walking by his house, he would never make eye contact. For months, he would never even look my way as I would walk by his house. He would sit in a chair in front of his house smoking a cigarette. He also liked to take walks, so sometimes I would pass him on the sidewalk. He would walk far around me to avoid me. From time to time, he made eye contact and I would say "hello." Previously, I had an opportunity to give him a Bible tract that he accepted then quickly walked on. No opportunity to talk with him is given. Another time, I invited him and his family to our church for a special Old Fashion Sunday and told him about the food and fun for the children after the service.

This Halloween morning, I am walking toward him, as I have many times before and the Holy Spirit pricks my heart that this is the morning to talk to him. As we come face to face, I say, "May I ask you a question?" He stops and looks me in the face. I tell him I have wanted to ask him this for a long time. His curiosity is peaked. I ask, "If you were to get in a car wreck and die, do you know for sure you would go to heaven?" He says "Yes", as he starts to walk away and then I ask, "How do you know?" He says, "Because I believe in God; I think I would." He is walking away now and my opportunity has officially passed, but I do say, "It is all about Jesus and what He did." He looks me in the face and continues walking away. My heart sinks as he walks away because I want to tell him more about my Savior Jesus and how he can know for sure he will go to heaven.

My job is to keep on with working for Jesus in this life to benefit others in their next life no matter what is happening to me. I need to continue to tell others about Jesus and how He died for their sins and wants to be their Lord and Savior. I also need to seek ways to be an encouragement to others. I ask God, "How can I be an encouragement to someone today?" God will give me opportunities if I ask and am willing and bold enough to do as He asks to be a help to others. "Rejoice evermore" means that God is in control and my job is to trust and believe and "keep on keeping on."

Opening our mailbox, I see there is a letter with my husband's doctor's name on it. He told me they were mailing it for us to see. I take it inside and set it down on the table while I proceed to open the rest of the mail. I wait a few moments and then I finally pick up the letter, open it, and read the lab results. As I read through each result, I mark down what each result is and if it is high or low. I make a copy of the two sheets and then highlight each result that is abnormal and also those that are right on the edge of being abnormal results. The page starts to look like the sun's yellow rays are shining through the paper because my yellow highlighter is all over both pages.

Being a nurse, of course I research each result and realize all of the problems that could be happening. Thoughts of possible outcomes that could follow in a month when his blood will be tested again seem to overwhelm my mind. Andy had asked that we not tell people now, so I felt like I was carrying this burden alone because I didn't want to add more stress to my husband. I seek God's face and tell Him I want His will, whatever it may be.

The trials of cancer have been put upon many people in my life. What impresses me most is when I see those who suffer such pain and misery find the strength in their Savior to be an encouragement to others and still lift up the name of Jesus. I have seen my own husband, my daddy, and my mother-in-law live through cancer surgery and treatments. I saw a strength that I had not seen before in them. They shined with courage that no matter what they had to face that they would be an encouragement to others and give God glory through it all. One Sunday morning, we asked our class to pray for us, but gave them no specifics. One never knows what kind of a burden another person is carrying on his or her shoulders. That day I thanked my husband for encouraging me through his lesson and we took off our burden and gave it fully to Jesus to carry for us.

Philippians 4:7 says, "*And the peace of God, which passeth all understanding, shall keep your hearts and minds through Christ Jesus.*" In two weeks, Andy will have his blood tested again. I have decided that whatever the results of the tests are, we will face it together when the time comes. Instead of allowing worry, fear, insecurity, hopelessness, and negativity to overcome me, I am using the armor of God to overcome. As I pray with the helmet of salvation, the breastplate of righteousness, the loins of truth, my feet shod with the preparation of the gospel of peace, the shield of faith and the sword of the Spirit, I am encouraged that I can defeat anything that comes at us with God as our Protector.

God uses situations throughout our lives to prepare us for our future spiritual battles. I have faced many hardships, but I thank God for each one because it is through them that I have grown closer to Him. One of my biggest fears as a young mother was becoming a widow with three small children to rear alone. My sons are now ages 20, 18, and 17. I know that whatever happens, I will take life one step at a time.

As usual, I woke up early this morning. I made my coffee, looked at Facebook, and laid out our devotional books for family devotions. I woke up the boys and told them it was time for family devotions. When my husband walked into the living room, I saw extreme exhaustion on his face. His color was not the best either. We started our reading and took turns as we usually do. He had the last turn; but looked at me with a face that said he didn't have the strength. I asked Tim to finish reading the chapter for his father. Andy called work to see if he could stay home, but he had meetings that he couldn't miss. I gave him some cold water and walked him to his car. I hugged him goodbye and told him, "I love you, have a great day."

His anemic look stirred my heart to text my family and friends for prayer for a special unspoken. We have not told anyone about his blood work results yet. He plans to wait until the end of the month to get his blood work tested again. He doesn't want his Thanksgiving holiday ruined by bad news. So, we wait. Waiting is one of the hardest lessons out there. I want to know the answer so we can plan our next step. I was reading about how Abraham and Sarah were told they would have a son. Instead of waiting on the Lord, they used their handmaid, Hager, to have a son, Ishmael. The descendants of Ishmael and Isaac have been fighting ever since. I am learning to wait on the Lord because I know He knows the best way for my life. I am praying that whatever happens, for God to get all the glory.

Today we were told that Andy's test results had not improved, so the doctor ordered another lab test to be completed in three months. We are continuing on with our lives trusting God's will. God is giving us strength and health as we need it. We are rejoicing evermore because "God is good all the time".

Rejoice evermore. In everything give thanks: for this is the will of God in Christ Jesus concerning you. 1 Thessalonians 5:16, 18

CHAPTER 14

NO NEGATIVE THOUGHTS OR TALK ALLOWED

Whether therefore ye eat, or drink, or whatsoever ye do, do all to the glory of God.
1 Corinthians 10:31

Most women, if not all, have had times when they were depressed whether momentarily or for long periods of time. God has given women hormones which will send us on a tail spin if we allow them to. It is important to keep our feelings, thoughts, and words in check.

If women allowed themselves to express every feeling inside of them, within minutes, she might experience sadness, happiness, and anger. She may be crying and when asked, "What's wrong?" the only answer given is "I don't know" and she is being truthful.

It is very important that we do not allow negative thoughts to assail and control us. We must be on guard as to what we permit into our thought life. If we allow negativity to constantly berate us, we will start to believe the lying words as truth. The best way to know truth is to know God's Word and use it as a lie detector. If what we hear or think disagrees with what God's Word says, then we know it is a lie.

It is wise to test each thought we have by God's Word. If it hurts us or puts us down in any way, then we know it is not a thought that we should be "listening" to. By reading and memorizing God's Word, we prepare ourselves to be on the offensive toward negative thoughts. God's Word is our Sword of the Spirit and is our weapon to use against opponents who wish to harm us.

Negative thoughts will continue to pile up to the point that we have taken our problem and made a mountain out of a mole hill. We choose to believe the worst case scenario is what will happen to us each time we have a tragedy. As I look back over my life and think of the tragedies I have faced, I can think of one time that the worst case scenario did happen; but I am so thankful today because it was through the passing of my dad that I was brought closer to God. I would not have learned to go to my heavenly Father and hold Him so close if my earthly father was still here. I have gained strength that only comes through experiencing great loss.

Through the many problems and tragedies I have faced, I see the hand of God at work in my life. I see how He took illness, cancer, and a car accident and used it for His glory. I was 20 years old when I was told I had endometriosis. If I had known that day that my pain would be with me increasing in intensity over the next 17 years, I really don't know if I could have dealt with it. God is so merciful to give us one day at a time. For approximately the next 5,840 days I would live with pain and/or being physically exhausted due to my endometriosis. I was able to take each day and allow God to work in my life for His glory. If I would have focused on the pain and allowed it to run my life with negative thoughts, I would not have been able to be used by God in a positive way over those years.

My husband and I were married for two years when he was diagnosed with cancer. Andy's cancer could have taken his life; but through God's providence, surgery, and radiation treatments, he has lived now for 25 more years since he was told he had cancer. We could have blamed God and asked why, but we chose to grow closer to God through this experience and trust Jesus to help us each step of the way. We made it through this time with a peace that God is in control of everything. Instead of having negative thoughts overtake our minds and discourage us, we chose to go on with life and allow God to work through us.

When our son, Timothy, was in an accident involving Andy's full-size truck, we thought tragedy had struck. We had just finished eating our delicious hamburgers and fries together at a local diner. As we went to our vehicles, I asked Tim if he wanted to drive the van or the truck and he chose the truck. Tim was broadsided while crossing a four-lane road. The truck was pushed across the road to the other side. The driver side door was smashed in all the way to the seat. I believe an angel kept the door from moving in another inch. If he had taken the van, I believe his left leg or perhaps whole left side would have been crushed. He was able to walk out of the truck and was completely uninjured except a little soreness from the impact.

When this accident happened, my husband was out of town, so I had to handle dealing with the insurance, etc. I was determined to look for the blessing in this tragedy. My husband loved his truck, so it was a big loss to him. The truck was considered totaled by the insurance company, so we were able to use the money to buy a small car that had much better gas mileage. When our son Jacob graduated from UCF and was headed to West Coast Baptist College for Pastoral Studies, we were able to give him the car to take with him. He and his dad drove from Florida to California in a very memorable trip that neither will ever forget.

Anytime hardship hits us and turns our world upside down, we need to look for blessings that will soon be coming. As we ride the wave instead of allowing it to knock us down, we can learn and gain so much more through everything that we face. Thinking negatively keeps us from rejoicing and seeing God's blessings. Are you facing a tragedy today? Thank God right now for the blessing He will soon be sending your way.

Another problem Christians face is falling into sin and not realizing how they got there. We must have a plan to avoid sin and when caught up in it, to stop and flee immediately, so our testimonies for God are not ruined. Sin starts in the mind. We start thinking about how nice it would be to have friends and to just hang out with them. We feel lonely and see no problem hanging out with some unsaved coworkers. We talk ourselves into thinking that it is ok and we are strong enough not to commit the same sins they do. This is step 1. We allow our thoughts to move to the point of thinking nothing is wrong with socializing with those who are living in continual sin. Step 2 is where we go out or hang out with them in places where we feel comfortable and safe. Maybe we go "putt-putt" golfing with them and they seem a lot like us. Next, they invite us out to a restaurant that has a bar. We are also comfortable with this because we know that they drink, but we won't. We may even agree to be their designated driver. Because we are not drinking, this drives them crazy and makes them feel a little guilty. It then becomes their new goal in life to see you drink also. They gang up on you and constantly tell you how nice a drink would be or how much you deserve it because of the hard work week you had. Step 3 is where you should stand up and tell them goodbye and leave, never to hang out with them again. So many will stay and be talked into the drink and hurt their testimony for Jesus Christ. They see us doing the same sins as them, so we are not so very different. Step 4 is where we give up and become just like them. We sound like them, dress like them, and act like them. On the other hand, we can confess our sins and set ourselves apart from the world and start over with a new slate and new mercies from God. *I beseech you therefore, brethren, by the mercies of God, that ye present your bodies a living sacrifice, holy, acceptable unto God, which is your reasonable service. And be not conformed to this world: but be ye transformed by the renewing of your mind, that ye may prove what is that good, and acceptable, and perfect, will of God.* Romans 12:1-2

It is imperative to make a plan not to socialize with the world or worldly Christians so as to not fall into continual habitual sins that ruin a Christian's testimony and perhaps their life. First, do not hang out with unsaved people or worldly Christians in socializing situations. Second, sin starts in the mind; do not allow your thought processes to lead you into continual sin. Third, stay in God's Word and pray daily. Fourth, find scripture verses that apply to your problem area and meditate on them. Fifth, realize that the worldly and carnal Christians hate feeling guilty about their sins, so their goal will be to trip you up to make you just like them. Sixth, find someone to hold you accountable daily. Seventh, it is easier to avoid temptation than it is to get out of the sin trap once you fall into it. Flee from temptation like Joseph did in the Bible. He did not stay, he ran away to avoid sin. Do not go to places or be with people where temptation is always lurking. If this plan is followed, it will keep you from falling into sin pits.

For I reckon that the sufferings of this present time are not worthy to be compared with the glory which shall be revealed in us. Romans 8:18

CHAPTER 15

TEEN STRUGGLES

Lo, children are an heritage of the LORD: and the fruit of the womb is his reward.
Psalm 127:3

Sometimes in our lives, we have to go through hardship to grow spiritually. If one of our sons has a foot that is infected with gangrene, we would be horrible parents to stick a Band-Aid over it, give him a crutch, and agree that it would be fine. Truthfully, he needs to go to the hospital and have it treated or even amputated so he will not die. Antibiotics are needed along with time for healing. It will be a painful, long process if the foot is amputated; but we as parents will be with him through it all. Even if he thinks we are being mean because it hurts so much, it must be done. We must look down the road to where he is alive, healed from infection, and walking again with a prosthetic foot. At the end of that road he has become strong and healthy and is thankful to us for doing what was right even if at the time he saw us as the enemy because of the pain.

A personal example in our family's life was when Tim had a "long boarding" accident going down a very steep hill. It gave him a gash on his face where his glasses were torn off, an arm with "road rash", a raw knee, and the worst part, a right palm completely void of skin. We used salve, bandages, and antibiotics to aid in the healing process and protect the hand from infection. Over the next few weeks, as his mom and nurse, I spent much time taking off old bandages, applying salve, adding new bandages, wrapping the hand in ace bandages, making sure he took his oral antibiotic, Ibuprofen, and Tylenol as needed. I also had to sometimes help him dress.

He could not use his right hand for a while. He also was not able to work. We had to rearrange the appointment time we had made for his senior pictures because he was so badly hurt. As the tasks were time-consuming and sometimes frustrating taking care of Tim, I knew it was necessary for him to completely heal. I am amazed at our bodies and their healing processes. Within a few weeks, God healed Tim's body with new skin. Going through it was difficult, but the result was so worth the pain. He is now healed, working again, and able to use his right hand as if nothing happened.

The hardest part of parenting teens is doing what is right in the long run. Most teens don't have the wisdom to see past their own faces. We must protect them now and in the future. Our teens are stronger than we think. God is molding the Christian teenager for his future. We must be careful not to run in as parents and try to make it easier for them. Like a baby bird struggling to get out of his egg, if he is helped, his wing muscles will not develop and he will not be able to fly later. We must let them struggle so they can fly in the future.

As a mother of three sons, I have learned that it is part of life for them to feel pain, disappointment, rejection, heartache, and even failure. I have learned so much more from the negative times in my own life than from my successes. I think of Peter who denied even knowing Jesus. When Jesus looked at him as the rooster crowed, Peter experienced firsthand disappointing his Savior and friend. I know Peter must have said to himself, "I don't care if I have to die for Jesus, I will never deny and disappoint Him again." It hurts for a mom to watch her child in pain, but as he grows closer to God through hard times, he becomes stronger spiritually. If you want independent, spiritually strong men as sons, you need to allow them to experience the pains of life without coddling them. Comfort and encourage them; apply God's Word and bandage with prayer; cry out to God for protection and then trust God to take care of them. I have to mentally hold myself back at times because the "Mama Bear" inside of me wants to protect. I use this energy in prayer. God's ways are so much better than our ways. As Corrie Ten Boom's visual example of embroidery shows us, God sees the beauty of the completed embroidery while all we see is the chaos of the backside. Therefore, I have become a prayer warrior mom. Of course we are right beside them through whatever they are going through. We do need to allow them to have some independence to become the godly men God intends them to be. Whether you have sons or daughters, allowing them to have some independence and grow from life's trials will be a huge help to their development as godly men and women in their futures.

Our son Timothy was blessed to be able to preach on what would have been my dad's 93rd birthday if he were living. It was such a blessing to hear our son preach with such passion that I knew the Holy Spirit was working through him. I was very encouraged and my heart was pricked to become a bolder Christian no matter what happens to me in the life ahead of me. I was also challenged to be a better witness for Jesus. Tim has become a great leader and I know God is going to use his life mightily as a missionary spreading the Gospel of Jesus.

Some days are very burdensome with teens and you may feel like you are not making a difference in their lives. One thing I have witnessed as a teacher and a parent is that children and/or teens sometimes appear as though they do not comprehend what you are trying to teach them. Days later when they act a certain way or say something that you have taught them, it encourages you that it is all worthwhile.

As parents, we are molding our most important treasures of stewardship given to us temporarily from God. Our actions and time spent today cultivating and developing our children will bear fruit in all the years ahead. What our children act like now is likely the same way they will act as adults. May God give us all strength and endurance to hold fast now so we can be abundantly blessed in our silver years and with our grandchildren who will also be a Godly inheritance to bring forth joy.

A good man leaveth an inheritance to his children's children: and the wealth of the sinner is laid up for the just. Proverbs 13:22

CHAPTER 16

INVITING JESUS TO BE PART OF OUR DAY

But rather seek ye the kingdom of God; and all these things shall be added unto you.
Luke 12:31

My morning began with me starting the laundry, making coffee, checking Facebook, and then sitting down in my rocker recliner to drink my coffee and to read my Bible and pray. As I was throwing dirty clothes into the washing machine, I was inspired to sing to my Savior to comfort my troubled heart. I sang, "Jesus is the Lighthouse" and "My God is so big, so strong and so mighty, there is nothing that He cannot do for you." The day is October 1, 2013, day one of the government shutdown which means my husband is at home without pay.

A few minutes into reading God's Word, I am interrupted with a phone call. My heart gets all excited thinking the furlough has all been taken care of and he is being told to go back to work. My husband takes the call. Afterwards, I walk into our bedroom and ask my husband what the call was about. He says it is the official call to let him know to stay home. My heart sunk a little, but then I just went back to my Bible reading and prayer knowing that no matter what, God will take care of His children His way.

Thanking God for the phone call, I decide that I will be excited to watch God's hand at work in dealing with our needs over the next few days, weeks, months, or years. Although I do not know what the futures holds for my family, I do know and trust that my Savior, Jesus Christ, will go through it with us. I am thankful today for an early morning phone call because God is in control regardless of the odds we face.

My goal is to invite Jesus to be part of my day every morning. The Holy Spirit is always with me and is my encourager and comforter. As I sing to Jesus and read or say God's Word in my mind, I am inviting my Lord and Savior to be part of my day. As I take worry and throw it on the ground and stomp on it, it fades away. I don't need to worry because I trust the Savior of my soul with the problems of my life. He created me and saved my soul from Hell when He died on the cross for the sins of the world. I know I can trust Him with providing my needs and taking care of me.

Many times in our lives, the tests or trials we face seem like Mount Everest. There seems to be no way out of the situation. God's ways are so much better than our ways. As I list out my specific needs to God in my prayer journal, I know it is so small (but not unimportant) to Him. My God is so much bigger than my troubles. I look forward to His way of providing for us and seeing the faith of our family increased. Tragedy and hardship brings bonding. I see this in our sons. When they are so giving and selfless, it brings joy to a mom's heart.

Today marks the end of the first week my husband has been on furlough. It has been easy so far because we had the money to pay off our monthly bills. Looking ahead, there is no light at the end of the tunnel. We decide that gas will be the only expense we will charge because there are certain places that we need to be able to drive to. I sat down and wrote some specific needs on my prayer list. As I invited Jesus to be part of my day, I asked first that my husband would be able to return to his job with back pay. Next, I started listing specific needs for our family: laundry detergent, dish detergent, milk, money to pay our bills next month, gas money, food to eat, car payments, electricity, water, etc. As I look over the amount of money we will need, I know the task ahead is impossible for us; but I have a God that deals with "impossible" all the time. We trust Him to take care of all of our problems.

Tonight, we will have an at home date night. I plan to cook spaghetti, make salad, and toast garlic bread. We will get a movie from the library and enjoy a night at home without much expense. Our youngest son will be working at McDonalds, so we will invite our middle son, Tim, to join us. We are looking for ways we can be good stewards. We know God will have to rescue us with money, food, gas, and miscellaneous necessities.

We take so much for granted: a paycheck that we use to pay our bills each month, food that we buy every week from the grocery store, and date night that we enjoy weekly. From this experience, I will have empathy and truly understand how it feels to be without an income for the family. God has laid it on my heart that when this is finished for our family, there will be ways we can help those in our church who are unemployed, have health problems, or have had financial hardship. I have learned how important it is to make sure those who are unemployed have their needs supplied also.

Many local churches have food pantries. This has taught me that food is not the only necessary item families have need of. I pray about how God would have our family be an encouragement to other families when the furlough is over.

Today begins week two of our furlough. It was somewhat stressful as I fought the temptation to worry. As I look at the amount of money needed for our bills, gasoline, food, electricity, water, I know that my "faith muscle" is truly getting a workout. As my prayer warrior partner recently told me, I also am telling my troubles, "God is much bigger than you are." I trust Him to provide all of our needs.

As I woke up this morning, God placed scripture verses on my heart reminding me that He will take care of me and my family. Matthew 10:29-31 says, "*Are not two sparrows sold for a farthing? And one of them shall not fall on the ground without your Father. But the very hairs of your head are all numbered. Fear ye not therefore, ye are of more value than many sparrows.*" These verses comfort and remind me that God is in control and that He can have a bird bring us food like he did for Elijah if necessary. I am praying that God will place our family on peoples' hearts and they will bring us food, money, gas cards, and anything that we will need that I cannot think of. I want to see the hand of God at work in our lives.

Our oldest son is going to Bible College to be a pastor; our middle son will go to Bible College next year to be a Missionary; our youngest son will also attend Bible College before moving back home to become a Mechanical Engineer. I see God working in each of their lives to prepare them for their futures. If they can learn to trust God completely with all of their needs, He will be able to use their lives for His glory so much more.

Luke 12:22-31 says, "*And He said unto His disciples, Therefore I say unto you, Take no thought for your life, what ye shall eat; neither for the body, what ye shall put on. The life is more than meat, and the body is more than raiment. Consider the ravens: for they neither sow nor reap; which neither have storehouse nor barn; and God feedeth them: how much more are ye than the fowls? And which of you with taking thought can add to his stature one cubit? If ye then be not able to do that thing which is least, why take ye thought for the rest? Consider the lilies how they grow; they toil not, they spin not; and yet I say unto you that Solomon in all his glory was not arrayed like one of these. If God then so clothe the grass, which is today in the field, and tomorrow is cast into the oven; how much more will He clothe you, O ye of little faith? And seek not ye what ye shall eat, or what ye shall drink, neither be ye of doubtful mind. For all these things do the nations of the world seek after: and your Father knoweth that ye have need of these things. But rather seek ye the kingdom of God; and all these things shall be added unto you.*" I am so encouraged by God's Word. He knows all of our needs. He will provide them for us when we need them. Grace is when God gives us what we need when we need it and in the right amount.

Gaining empathy for those who are going through hard times, I thank

God for this opportunity to be without so I can truly understand. As I learn from my experiences and gain knowledge of the best ways to help others in need, I ask God to go before me and give me wisdom.

We had a friend from our church who gave us a turkey; it was very kind of her and very much appreciated by our family. One of our singles in our Sunday school class invited our family over to her and her family's home for dinner tonight. God is providing in many ways for us.

Before this furlough began, I sent $10 McDonald's gift cards to several young people. God laid it on my heart to encourage them. One thing I have learned by having the gift of giving, is that God gives back to you over and over again so much more than you give. Our family recently gave $400 to some young people that God laid on our hearts. Each member of our family gave towards this gift. I cannot wait to see all the many ways God will give back to us. I like to give birthday gifts and cards to the Singles in our Sunday school class and to others God leads me to give to. I do not have to worry or fear because God will not be out given and He takes care of the needs of His children.

Earlier this week, I was struggling with how God was going to take care of all of our many needs. As I kept thinking of more and more bills and responsibilities, it was becoming harder to stop worrying. So I sent my prayer partner and fellow prayer warrior a text asking her to please send me a Bible verse that I could meditate on. She sent back two verses: Isaiah 43:2 and Isaiah 44:2. She said she kept trying to send Isaiah 43:2, but her phone kept pulling up Isaiah 44:2. After several times of it doing this, she finally decided to see what the verse said. She felt that this was the verse God wanted me to have, so she sent both.

As I received the verses, I pulled up the verses on my Bible application and tried to send the two verses to my phone message center so I could easily pull them up and read them daily. I sent Isaiah 44:2 easily and went back to send the other verse. I tried again and again, but was never able to send the second verse. I finally gave up and realized Isaiah 44:2 was the verse God wanted me to live by during this time of faith and trusting Him. Later my prayer partner and I talked about this and I realized how the hand of God was leading me directly to this verse: Isaiah 44:2 *"Thus saith the Lord that made thee, and formed thee from the womb, which will help thee; Fear not, O Jacob, my servant; and thou, Jesurun, whom I have chosen."* What I took from this verse was that I need to remember that God created everything and He will help me. Also, I do not need to fear at all. I am His servant and I have been chosen by Him to do something amazing and wonderful with my life. I happily look forward to the way God will use my life for His glory.

Praise the Lord the furlough has now ended and we are now receiving paychecks again for which we are extremely grateful. God provided for all of our needs His way. Our family has grown spiritually from seeing God's hand at work. I have become much more empathetic to those who are unemployed or going through hard times. God laid it on the hearts of my husband and I to do a Christmas project this year for five families in our church providing those with items that are not readily available and are needed when having financial hardship. Our whole Singles Sunday school class became involved also by providing items for our gift bags for these families. I enjoyed seeing the spiritual growth of our Singles who cheerfully gave to others in need.

It was such a blessing to deliver the Christmas gift bags. The first bag went to a family with a mom that has had a lot of health problems this year. The family was so thankful and asked us to thank the class also. The second family was a man who is shut-in at a nursing home due to health. Our sons and I went through every item in the basket and showed it to him. He was so thankful and gracious. Bringing joy to him brought so much joy to my heart personally. The third and fourth families had loss of jobs this year. They were both so thankful and appreciative. We were given a "thank you" note to read to the entire class. The fifth family had multiple hospitalizations this year. They were so very thankful and surprised that a class full of singles would have the compassion to give to others. It truly is so much "more blessed to give than to receive." The entire Singles class was truly blessed by being able to give from our hearts joyfully this Christmas.

The furlough has brought many life lessons. I am thankful for life lessons no matter how hard they are because they will forever be branded into my heart as a remembrance of how and what we can do for others. I have learned once again that one cannot out give God, and it truly is more blessed to give than to receive.

The steps of a good man are ordered by the LORD: and he delighteth in his way.
Psalms 37:23

CHAPTER 17

ACHIEVING MORE

Study to shew thyself approved unto God, a workman that needeth not to be ashamed, rightly dividing the word of truth. 2 Timothy 2:15

"Shoot for the stars." "Aim for the moon and even if you fall short, you will land among the stars." I have heard these sayings throughout my lifetime. One should set his goal high and even if the goal is not reached, he will achieve much. Our youngest son Caleb took the SAT college entrance exam. He wanted to score high enough to be offered scholarships, but his score was just a little low. My sister teaches SAT Prep classes and had an opening for the summer class. My husband and I decided that Caleb and I would go stay with my sister for the two week class. It was a fast-paced class that equaled the amount of time spent in a semester.

At first, Caleb resisted and did not want to do it because it would take two weeks of his last summer before he graduates from high school. He knew the amount of time he would be investing and did not want to do it at first. Once he started the class and was learning testing techniques, he saw what an asset this class could be to his score. Caleb is the type of person that if he makes something his goal, he will give it 110%. He made this class his goal. He plans on incorporating test practicing over the next two months to keep what he has learned fresh so he can improve his test score.

Caleb took his SAT exam on Saturday, October 5, 2013. He hoped to increase his score by 150 to 250 points. He increased his overall score by 330 points! He surpassed his goal and was amazed at this accomplishment.

People need to reach for goals beyond what they think they can do. We need to try to go above and beyond what we think we can do because often we are much more capable than we give ourselves credit for.

After applying for a scholarship, we realized that he was 20 points too low for Florida home school students. As a home school student, the state will not accept any transcript from a parent. He would need to have taken all of his courses at Florida virtual school or from a community college. He would need to have had four math, four English, four history, and four science classes from the community college or virtual school. Since he began dual enrollment this past year, he has not accomplished this task.

Talking to the scholarship representative, I was told to have him focus on just one segment, like Math, and increase that score by the 20 points above his highest score. We have one chance left for him to take the SAT for the scholarship. I explained to Caleb that if he increased his score, this scholarship would be worth approximately $11,000 - $14,000. He has eleven weeks in order to prepare by taking the math tests from the College Board SAT Prep book.

He has taken a couple of practice tests and is scoring well. He is scoring 40-50 points higher on the math section than he has done before. We, as his parents, are encouraging him to learn from each problem he misses to help increase his score. His dad is reviewing any missed questions with him. We will encourage him to continue learning and watching God bless him for his effort.

We received his SAT scores for his May 3rd test and he did score the 20 points higher he needed; unfortunately, his points were in Math and Writing instead of Math and Reading. Therefore, he is 10 points (the equivalent of one missed question) short of the needed points to receive the scholarship as a home school student. I am proud of Caleb for trying one last time to achieve more. This closes certain doors so we thank God for His leading in this way. God is good all the time and always provides for what He asks His children to do.

Let your light so shine before men, that they may see your good works, and glorify your Father which is in heaven. Matthew 5:16

CHAPTER 18

GOD IS GIVER OF ALL GOOD THINGS

For God so loved the world, that he gave his only begotten Son, that whosoever believeth in him should not perish, but have everlasting life. John 3:16

Each one of us is different in a variety of ways. We all have different finger prints, personalities, and goals in life. Psalm 139:14 says, *"I will praise Thee; for I am fearfully and wonderfully made: marvelous are thy works; and that my soul knoweth right well."* God created each one of us as unique individuals, but also with many similarities. We all have the five senses of seeing, hearing, smelling, tasting, and touching. We also all have the ability to think with the amazing computer brain God gave to each of us.

We are blessed with the ability to see from the day we are born. Our eyes take in so much more than we realize to be stored in our brain. I like to walk and bike ride in my neighborhood. I am blessed every morning with a blended assortment of colors in the morning sky. Most every day I thank God for giving us color to enjoy. Can you imagine if everything we saw was only in shades of black and grey? I know many deaf people that do not hear, but their eyes become so much more observant and they are able to comprehend what is happening around them even if no one is using sign language. A lot of our communication is not by word, but by sight of gestures or non-verbal communication.

Sitting on my sister's back porch this week, I have been able to enjoy the sounds of frogs croaking, birds chirping, and cats meowing. The gift of hearing allows us to appreciate a part of creation that makes life easier. If I take my glasses off at night, even though I cannot see across the room, I can still hear the TV and absorb what is happening. I am able to visualize the picture in my brain. Go outside around dusk and sit with your eyes closed. Focus on all of the different sounds and try to create a mental image of what is happening all around you.

The smell of coffee brewing woke me up this morning. This is one of my favorite smells. Some other wonderful smells are cookies in the oven, homemade soup on the stove, and roses in a vase. Smells bring back memories. The smell of a cake reminds me of afternoons spent at Grandma's home in the kitchen baking goodies.

One of my favorite movies is "Ratatouille." It is a movie about a rat that loves to cook. He has a passion for food. While his family eats garbage, he is at a neighbor's home searching her kitchen for spices to enhance the taste of whatever mushroom or herb he finds outside. My favorite scene is when he takes a strawberry and a chunk of cheese and takes a bite of each separately; then he takes a bite of the two together. Fireworks shoot off to visualize how amazing the taste is of the combination of these two foods. Sometimes, I will close my eyes when I take a bite of food in order for my whole attention to be on its taste. I also like to taste new foods to see if I like them. You never know if you will like something until you try it.

It has been determined that babies that are not touched by other humans may fail to thrive and eventually die. God has placed in us a need for other people and their touch. Have you ever heard someone say, "I just really need a hug today"? This is his way of saying he needs the comfort of human touch. I like to hug the older widow ladies in our church because I know they are without much human touch. Even as teenagers, one should be hugging his mom and dad each day and telling them he loves and appreciates them. This benefits both the teen and his parents.

Thinking is not one of the five senses, but it is an amazing gift from our Creator God. Our brain has the incredible ability to store and remember so much more than we can ever use. Paul Reber, Professor of Psychology at Northwestern University said in the Scientific American Mind April, 2010 journal, (6. Reber) "The human brain consists of about one billion neurons. Each neuron forms about 1,000 connections to other neurons, amounting to more than a trillion connections. If each neuron could only help store a single memory, running out of space would be a problem. You might have only a few gigabytes of storage space, similar to the space in an iPod or a USB flash drive. Yet neurons combine so that each one helps with many memories at a time, exponentially increasing the brain's memory storage capacity to something closer to around 2.5 petabytes (or a million gigabytes)." He continues to say this is an approximation, but it gives us an idea of how incredible the ability of our brain is.

With this gift from God, it is our responsibility to use it to the best of our ability for His glory. We should be making goals that exceed our abilities in our own minds and going for gold. So many people are satisfied with bronze when they are silver or gold in ability. My goal for a test is always to get 100%. I knew that I could not always get 100%, but that is my goal. My life verse is 1 Corinthians 10:31, *"Whether therefore ye eat, or drink, or whatsoever ye do, do all to the glory of God."* Our goal as Christians should always be to do our best for God's glory.

If you are not a Christian, the first thing you should do is realize that no one is good enough to get into heaven on their own merit. Romans 3:23 tells us *"For all have sinned and come short of the glory of God."* This means that no matter how good you are, you have at least one sin and that is all it takes to keep you out of heaven. For example, I heard a pastor tell it this way: Suppose you have five eggs and are making an omelet. You break four eggs and put them in a bowl. When you break the fifth egg, you find it is rotten. You say to yourself that it doesn't matter because you have four good eggs. In reality, we know that the one bad egg is all it takes to ruin the whole omelet. This is how it is with sin in our lives. Only one sin is enough to make us not perfect. Romans 6:23 says, *"The wages of sin is death, but the gift of God is eternal life through Jesus Christ our Lord."* The payment or price for our sin is death in hell. Jesus is the only way to avoid hell because we are not good enough to get to heaven on our own. He died on the cross for all of the sins of everyone. Jesus was beaten beyond recognition with a whip with nine tails that had objects like broken glass or metal pieces smashed into it. His beard was pulled out. He was nailed to the cross and died to pay the penalty for all sin. Romans 5:8 says, *"But God commended His love toward us in that while we were yet sinners, Christ died for us."*

It is up to each individual person to have faith in Jesus and all that He did for us and accept Him as Savior. He also rose from the grave three days later proving He is the Christ and Savior of the world. There were hundreds of people that saw Him after He rose again. Romans 10:13 says, *"Whosoever shall call upon the name of the Lord shall be saved."* When I was nine years old, I went to a church camp and listened to the preacher talk about how you could know for sure that when you die you could go to heaven. I was not sure, so I went back to my dorm and sat on my bunk bed. I prayed and told God that I believed in His Son Jesus, that He died on the cross for my sins, and rose from the dead three days later. I asked Jesus to forgive me of my sins and to save me. Now I know for sure that when I die I will go to heaven, not because of how good I am, but because of what Jesus did for me. My faith is in Him alone to save me with nothing added such as baptism, good works, or family ties.

God is such an incredible Creator. He decided every feature of your being from physical to mental to personality. He made you and you are His special masterpiece. We are wonderfully and marvelously made. It is our responsibility to use His gifts of salvation and creation for His glory.

Whether therefore ye eat, or drink, or whatsoever ye do, do all to the glory of God.
1 Corinthians 10:31

CHAPTER 19

ALWAYS GOD'S PRINCESS

Fear thou not; for I am with thee: be not dismayed; for I am thy God: I will strengthen thee; yea, I will help thee; yea, I will uphold thee with the right hand of my righteousness. Isaiah 41:10

Being away from my home and family is hard because I miss them. The benefit of the time apart is that I do not have to think about what their needs are ahead of mine. I do not have to cook, clean, or do any of the other million items on my mind that I feel need to be done. I am able to relax and not worry about anyone or anything.

My youngest son Caleb and I spent the past two weeks at my sister's home while he took an SAT Prep class at the local Christian School. After two weeks away from my husband and other two sons, I woke up feeling a little sad because I was starting to feel the stress of everything ahead of me at my home. I was hoping and praying my husband would make my sons clean up the house and kitchen. He is usually good about this, so I'm not too worried. I'm so looking forward to relaxing in my home with my family and I won't be able to relax if the house looks like a cyclone has hit it.

Instead of worrying and feeling stressed, God said to my heart that I am always His princess. As a wife and mom, I tend to lose who I am at times because I am so busy helping others that I don't get to just be myself. God's sweet reminder made me think that no matter what is happening, I am His princess and always will be. When I feel like I need someone to take care of or help me, I know He is always right beside me carrying me through whatever trial I am facing.

When bad things happen, we as Christians should automatically look up to God excitedly thinking about how He is going to bless us through our hard time. Jeremiah 29:11 tells us that God wants His best for us. 1 Corinthians 10:31 tells us to give God glory through everything in our lives. Our lives are adventures and we should ask God, "How may I give you glory today?"

The challenge is to become so close to God that whenever anything happens that is not what you expect or think would ever happen, you jump past all the thoughts of worry and fear and land directly in the arms of Jesus. Know that no matter what the circumstance, He is in control and you need not worry one little bit. It seems when I am able to deal with something well, the next unexpected wave that hits me is bigger and stronger. I know my Lord is trying to grow and stretch me to be more like Him. God is merciful and patient with me each time.

My husband will soon be getting his blood work rechecked after a month of waiting from the first set of bad results. Regardless of how bad or good the results may be, this past month of learning to lean on Jesus and Him alone has stretched me as His daughter and I have grown closer to Him than I have ever been. Instead of allowing worries to overtake and cripple me, I look forward to giving God glory through whatever trial lies ahead. He promises to never leave nor forsake me and I claim that promise.

Andy's results for his one month blood work came back out of the normal range. After months of waiting, Andy had his three months lab test results returned. His levels were within normal limits. Praise the Lord for his goodness. God is so good to answer prayers. Whatever you are facing today whether health problems, death of a loved one, or stress, learn to rejoice in the midst of the storm and ride the wave with Jesus by your side.

Let your conversation be without covetousness; and be content with such things as ye have: for he hath said, I will never leave thee, nor forsake thee. Hebrews 13:5

CHAPTER 20

GODLY CHARACTER IS IMPORTANT

Therefore if any man be in Christ, he is a new creature: old things are passed away; behold, all things are become new. 2 Corinthians 5:17

Why do children and teens believe they have rights that they do not have? You see a ten year old with a smart phone and his parents wonder why their son is never satisfied with anything he is given. We spoil our children to their detriment. Our sons did not get cell phones until they started dual enrolling at the local college. They appreciated the phone because they had to wait for it until they were starting college classes.

Children think it is Ok to live like slobs and not clean their rooms or help around the house with chores. Moms cannot do it all by themselves if they want to keep their health. A house runs so much smoother if everyone pitches in, helps, and does chores. The one person who usually does everything will appreciate the help because without it, life becomes overwhelming. It is important to teach your children how to clean up after themselves starting when they are able to put away their own toys. One of my favorite songs for my sons when they were little was "Clean up, clean up, everybody everywhere. Clean up, clean up, everybody do your share." They can help mom carry small items to show they are part of the team in their own home.

Mothers are burdened with responsibilities and expectations from everyone. She is expected to be the perfect supermom with chores such as: breakfast, lunch, and dinner prepared; washing, drying, and putting away dishes; washing, drying, and folding laundry; making sure the house clean at all times in case someone stops by; sweeping, mopping, and vacuuming the floors; washing, educating, buying for, baking for, and cooking for the children; supporting children by attending all games or whatever extracurricular activity each child is involved in; Changing diapers; feeding and playing with children; reading books; attending field trips and being in charge of four other kids other than your own; etc., etc.

Young "stay at home" moms should not be expected to be perfect. Having a perfect house may lead to ignoring our children. We can, on the other hand, choose to spend time with our children on important agendas such as: studying for a test, reviewing spelling words, playing a board game, eating lunch at McDonald's, playing catch with a baseball or Frisbee in the front yard, going on a bike ride, reading books that teach them character, talking about Bible stories, and having teaching moments when questions arise even if it is 11pm.

Building godly character in my sons' lives was much more important to me than mopping my floors every day. I feel successful as a mom when my sons defend what is right at the possibility of being ridiculed. I feel I have achieved when our sons choose abstinence until marriage and are proud of their virginity because they are obeying God. They know He will give them the wife that He has for them if they are just patient and wait on Him. I believe I have succeeded in teaching them well when my sons tell others about their Lord and Savior, Jesus Christ. Each of our sons has a goal for their future and trusts God to lead them. They all know that they must graduate from college and have a means of supporting their family before they get married. I have prayed for each of their future wives since my sons have been babies. Prayer works.

The next time you visit a home of a mom who has a three-year-old, a one-year-old, and a newborn, don't judge her because there are toys, games, and books scattered about her living room. She is teaching and her students are learning much. The laundry, dishes, and dust will be with us forever, but our children grow up and leave home. Cherish each moment no matter how chaotic because when they become adults, they will move away and they will live what you have taught them. I would be so much happier to have a son and daughter-in-law who have a chaotic home with love, learning, and laughter than for the home to be child-proofed, serious, and clean. What are you teaching your children to become as adults?

Finally, brethren, whatsoever things are true, whatsoever things are honest, whatsoever things are just, whatsoever things are pure, whatsoever things are lovely, whatsoever things are of good report; if there be any virtue, and if there be any praise, think on these things.
Philippians 4:8

CHAPTER 21

GOD'S MERCIES ARE NEW EVERY MORNING

It is of the Lord's mercies that we are not consumed, because His compassions fail not. They are new every morning: great is Thy faithfulness. The Lord is my portion, saith my soul; therefore will I hope in Him. The Lord is good unto them that wait for Him, to the soul that seeketh Him. It is good that a man should both hope and quietly wait for the salvation of the Lord. Lamentations 3:22-26

My heavenly Father is so compassionate and merciful. He shows His love to me with new mercies every morning. I do not deserve any mercy whatsoever; yet He gives it freely. People put very little thought and focus on others and what they can do for them. I send cards and give gifts to lift up hearts and encourage. Doing kind things for others actually brings joy to my heart. It truly is more blessed to give than to receive. If I never receive another gift, but I could give gifts to my heart's delight, I would be one joy-filled woman.

People have said that they wished they were spiritual enough to handle each of life's hard situations perfectly as soon as they happen. We are human and not perfect like Jesus. Our goal is not to be perfect because that is impossible; our goal should be to grow spiritually continually. Each life circumstance we face should teach and train us to better handle situations in our future. We are constantly being prepared by our heavenly Father to be our best for Him. He knows we are fragile. He also loves it when we come to Him, climb onto His lap, and cry out to Him knowing that He will take care of us and help us.

Growth to be more like Jesus Christ should be every Christian's goal.

God is merciful and understands we make mistakes and get tricked over and over again with the same temptation. He is there to teach us to watch for those pitfalls and learn to go around them instead of walking right into them. It is important to be watching out for Satan who has the goal to destroy you. One of my favorite verses that keeps me on the lookout is I Peter 5:8 *"Be sober, be vigilant; because your adversary the devil, as a roaring lion, walketh about, seeking whom he may devour."* We need to be in God's Word, praying, and seeking how we can give God glory in our lives. If we are busy about God's business seeking to please, praise, and thank Him, we will be less likely to fall so often into the same sins over and over again. Don't allow Satan to steal your joy no matter the circumstances or reasons. He cannot have a Christian's soul, so he goes for the next best thing, ruining your life and stealing your joy. Stay joyful in the Lord.

Is there anything you yearn for or lust after more than God? Do you desire chocolate cake or brownies, a sexy girl, a hunk of a guy, fame, money, success, or material items? Where are your time, attention, thoughts, and money spent? Are they spent on food, sex, pride of self, being rich, being boss, or next item on your must have list? Or are they on learning from God's Word which increases faith? Perhaps, your energies are spent on praying and knowing God will answer your prayers? Maybe you are thinking about someone you need to tell about Jesus and praying for the courage to talk to them knowing the boldness of the Holy Spirit will take over if you just take that first step. Are you spending one on one time alone with your Savior? Christians, the devil is working overtime to defeat all of us. His goal is to cripple us enough that we are useless as Christians and don't have faith enough to go to church, let alone tell others about Jesus. Growth as a Christian is never stagnant; we are always moving toward God or away from Him. It is time we wake up and realize the end is near. Christian, are you closer or further away from Jesus today than you were last week, month, or year?

O God, Thou art my God; early will I seek Thee; my soul thirsteth for Thee, my flesh longeth for Thee in a dry and thirsty land, where no water is. Psalm 63:1

CHAPTER 22

SHARKS IN OUR LIVES

Be sober, be vigilant, for your adversary the devil as a roaring lion walketh about seeking whom he may devour. 1 Peter 5:8

We will always have sharks in our lives. At times they are way out in the ocean and out of sight. Sometimes, they are circling us and we are not even aware they are there. We need to be on the lookout for temptations and pitfalls in our lives that will take a chunk of flesh out of us before we even realize it.

One summer my family took a vacation near the Sebastian Inlet in Florida. This inlet is known for shark sightings and shark bites. Along with the condo we rented, we were allowed access to a boat for the week. One morning we packed a picnic lunch and planned a day on the river in the boat. We spotted an island in the middle of the river and decided to stop and have our picnic lunch. As we finished eating, we spotted a dark hump on the sandbar nearby. We quickly loaded into the boat and sped off. We realized we had an alligator that was basking in the sun watching us have our picnic. Temptation is like that in the sense it is lying around near us. It is up to us to get as far away from it as possible and as fast as we can. If we stay near the temptation, it has a greater possibility of sneaking up on us and biting us.

The whole week in Sebastian was also "Shark Week" on TV. Every night, we would watch the shark stories. It is always interesting to hear firsthand accounts from shark bite survivors. Many faced a shark eye to eye while their arm was in its mouth; thinking that this was the last few moments of their lives. Some described their attack as a gentle bite that caused no pain whatsoever. When we imagine or see a video of a shark bite, it looks very painful. Seeing a Great White shark fully expose its teeth is one of the most frightening nightmares one could possibly have. Facing this shark in life brought horror to many swimmers. I believe the worst terror came when they finally got away and then needed to get to shore. It must have been petrifying not knowing where the shark was and if it would attack again at any moment.

One way to be sure not to be attacked by a shark is to stay out of the water. Sharks swim in oceans and in some rivers, so if you stay out of its territory, you will be safe. Our risk comes when we want to surf so badly that we decide to go into the water even though we know this area is known for sharks. In our lives, we should stay away from temptation. If we go to places where the temptation is, we certainly have a greater risk of falling into it. If you don't want to drink alcohol, stay away from bars or restaurants that serve it. If you are on a diet and losing weight, don't go to the bakery section and admire all of the sweets. If you have a tendency to lust after women, don't get on the computer and look at porn sites or watch movies with inappropriately dressed women. Temptation starts with the eyes seeing, followed by the mind and heart wanting, then yielding and finally committing the sin.

It is important and so helpful to make up your mind every morning that you are not going to commit sins that you have a tendency to do. You can decide that no matter what you are asked, you will not go to the bar with friends from work even just to be the designated driver. Plan ahead with the answer "no" and then stick to it. Staying a virgin until marriage doesn't come by hoping. It comes by standing on a firm decision and then not being alone in places where temptation could overcome you. My sons have purity rings symbolizing their commitment to remaining virgins until marriage. Our church did a "True Love Waits" ceremony with the teens and their parents. Marriage brings with it the luggage of the past sin life of both people. Sexual purity makes a firm foundation for a marriage.

Whatever stronghold you are facing, with the help of God, you can overcome it. You cannot hope or wish, but you must make a firm, "no exceptions" agreement to not do it. You must get in God's Word and find verses to help you when tempted. You must replace negative thoughts with verses, praise, and thanksgiving. God will give you strength, but you must determine you will do your part. Sharks will always be part of our lives because we live in an ocean that is surrounded with temptation. We must learn the ocean currents that we can swim in and also the deep, dark, cold trenches that we must avoid.

I can do all things through Christ which strengtheneth me. Philippians 4:13

CHAPTER 23

ONLY ONE WAY TO HEAVEN – SEEK JESUS

Ask, and it shall be given you; seek, and ye shall find; knock, and it shall be opened unto you: For every one that asketh receiveth; and he that seeketh findeth; and to him that knocketh it shall be opened. Matthew 7:7-8

At church in a children's class, I had a little girl come up to me and ask if she could be saved. My heart jumped for joy to see such strong faith in a child seeking Jesus as her Savior. I told her about Jesus and how He died on the cross for all the sins of the world and then rose from the dead three days later proving He is our risen Savior. It is through believing and having faith in Him and Him alone that brings salvation. After we finished talking, she said she wanted to receive Jesus as her personal Savior. We bowed our heads and she prayed a prayer of salvation. I asked her if she believed what she prayed with all of her heart and meant it. She said she did. I welcomed this young lady into the family of God.

The world today is self-centered and wants to do things its way. People do not like having anyone telling them what to do. They hate authority and want to be their own boss. They reject anything or anyone who tells them to submit. John 14:6 says, *"I am the Way, the Truth, and the Life. No man cometh unto the Father but by me."* The world does not want to hear that Jesus is the only way to heaven. How dare any religion try to be the only one; there should be all kinds of ways so everyone can do whatever they want or even do nothing. This corrupted way of thinking is what is leading a rebellious world to hell.

God's Word is Truth. From the creation of the world and the events of

Genesis, to the death and resurrection of Jesus Christ, to the last word, every word is true. Creation shouts loudly that there is a Creator. The intricate design of every living cell shows God's handiwork. The veins on a leaf, the petals on a flower, the waves of the ocean, the clouds in the sky, the grandeur of the mountains, the life cycle of a butterfly, the uniqueness of a platypus, the neurons of the human brain, all were created by God.

Nature in all of its wonders and complexity shout to everyone that it was created by God. He took six days to do His handiwork and rested on the seventh day. From light to firmament; to grass and trees; to sun, moon, and also the stars; to fish of the sea and birds of the air; to land animals and man; God created them all. He wants us to seek Him. He will show Himself to all who truly want to know Him and seek Him. Like the little girl saved at church who sought God to be her Savior with all of her heart, every person must seek Jesus Christ and have faith in Him alone to be saved.

When thou saidst, Seek ye my face; my heart said unto thee, Thy face, LORD, will I seek. Psalm 27:8

CHAPTER 24

UNDONE

So that I might finish my course with joy, and the ministry, which I have received of the Lord Jesus, to testify the gospel of the grace of God. Acts 20:24b

I asked the Lord to give me one word to write about today and He gave me the word "Undone" which means "not finished". The Lord is not finished with me yet. My "to do" list that I write in the morning never seems to get completely done. I wear many hats as a woman, a few being: mom, wife, home school teacher, writer, discipleship teacher/mentor, and Sunday school teacher's secretary and assistant. My goal is to continue working until God's work for me on earth is done. I know the type of work God has me do will change throughout the stages of my life.

As I turn to read the clock, I am astonished it is almost 11 am. I read my Bible, prayed, walked 2.3 miles, read a few pages in a couple of books, ate breakfast, had my cup of coffee, showered and dressed, washed two loads of laundry, and I am now sitting at my laptop writing this chapter. I see all I have done and realize that I have accomplished quite a bit. My prayers will be heard and answered. My Bible reading will be blessed. My walking has already energized me and cleared the cobwebs in my brain. My breakfast and coffee have given me vigor. My reading has awakened my mind to pondering the words I have read. My shower has refreshed me. My bed is made with freshly washed linens. Since sitting down at my laptop, I began a chapter from the one word that God gave me and am also encouraged that my goal is for everything I do to bring God glory.

Women need to realize all that they accomplish in a day. As a mom of toddlers, it seemed as if nothing was being done around the house while my husband was at work. My three-year old, one–year old, and newborn baby kept me quite busy. I had three in diapers for a short time. Breastfeeding the baby, feeding the two toddlers breakfast and lunch, changing all three of their diapers several times, cleaning up all of their messes, washing all of the dirty laundry for five people, putting the three boys down for naps, reading and playing with them, details only a few of my daily tasks at that time in my life. Moms should write down every task they do in a day and share it with their husbands. Or, even more memorable, have dad stay home for a full day with the children while you take a mommy's day off. He should never complain again, with the new found insight he gains.

God gives us passions according to how He wants to use our lives. I have three personal passions: writing, speaking in public to encourage, and teaching. I have taught for the last ten years. Now I feel God leading me to take the wisdom I have been given over the last 47 years and give it to others to encourage and warn them. As a mentor to young ladies, I feel it is my God ordered responsibility to lead and direct them in godly ways.

As my two youngest are high school seniors and dual enrolled at the local State College, I have decided to take this year and write the book I have always wanted to write. I finally have the time to give attention to my calling. Many people have been supportive of my goal and they tell me so. Some have not seen this book as a reality or possibility and they think it is a waste of time. My mind is made up and my goal is set. I will stand strong and continue to pursue my God-inspired mission. I am excited to see His hand in my life as He opens doors to my writing this book and speaking to ladies retreats and conferences. As God opens doors, I will proceed through them.

Being confident of this very thing, that he which hath begun a good work in you will perform it until the day of Jesus Christ. Philippians 1:6

CHAPTER 25

VISION

Where there is no vision, the people perish: but he that keepeth the law, happy is he.
Proverbs 29:18

Having a vision for your life is looking ahead with a general idea of what you want to accomplish in your life. With a clear vision, you next need to work to make it come to pass. My vision is to write this book and finish it by June. I prayed about it, set a goal, made a schedule, and now I am working toward my goal by writing.

If you do not have a clear vision, you probably will not set goals and your life will subsequently meander about from day to day. You need to make plans of how to reach your goals. A teenager may wish to become a Mechanical Engineer, but unless he plans and set goals, that desire will not be accomplished. He must first finish high school with good grades so he can go to college. His SAT scores must be high enough to get into a college. Once he is in college, he must choose the correct classes each semester to meet the guidelines for graduation. He must study and do all the projects so he can complete the classes with passing grades. He must apply for graduation for his college transcripts to be analyzed to see if he has completed all tasks necessary for graduation. He must make a resume and then send it out to many companies in order to get interviews. At the interview he must successfully present himself and his accomplishments in order to be seen as the best candidate for the position. Then, he will be offered the job of a mechanical engineer.

So many teenagers dream big but are not willing to put forth the effort to accomplish the tasks necessary to achieve. I recommend dreaming and dreaming big. You will not achieve more than you are willing to dream. You also cannot depend on others to do the hard work for you; you must do it yourself. Parents become cheerleaders and encouragers, but the task is the child's alone to meet.

When I was a child, my daddy was a mechanic and my momma was a stay-at-home mom. Neither of my parents had a college education, so a college degree was not impressed upon us as children. I find it interesting that both my sister and I have college educations and we have worked hard to ensure and encourage our children to get college educations as well. My husband and I taught our children growing up that after high school, you graduate from college and acquire a job to support your family before you get married. College is just another step in the lives of our children because they were taught how important it is.

Our youngest son Caleb works at a fast food restaurant and does a great job. We have heard encouraging remarks from his boss on how hard he works. We have taught him to have the work ethic of a day's pay for a good day's work. He is saving money for college through this job. He is so blessed to have it, but it has taught him that he does not want to work earning minimum wage for the rest of his life. He will make several times as much per hour as he earns now when he begins his job as a mechanical engineer.

It is the responsibility of the parents to encourage their children to dream, go to college, and become financially independent adults. I understand that some people are not made for college. My brother, James, was not able to go to college due to learning disabilities; but he has become the best in the area that God has placed him. He recently earned an award from his county for "Volunteer of the Year." He volunteers in a Senior Citizen Center and is loved and adored by the residents there. He does his best where God has placed him and he touches the lives of many people and encourages them.

After my dad died, my mom had three children to take care of with only an eighth grade education. We lived on my dad's social security and food stamps along with my mom's few earned dollars from babysitting. Seeing the position my mom found herself in with my dad's death, it became imperative to me that I get a college education as a woman and be able to adequately provide for my family if my husband died. I am grateful to my mom for all she did for us. She had a giving heart and loved us so much. We had a home, a car, clothes, food, and love. She is to this day the strongest woman I know and I admire her for being strong for her children.

Success does not just happen; it must be dreamed, planned, and achieved. All of these actions take courage, determination, and hard work. If you are going to dream, you might as well DREAM BIG!

When the LORD *turned again the captivity of Zion, we were like them that dream. Then was our mouth filled with laughter, and our tongue with singing: then said they among the heathen, The* LORD *hath done great things for them. The* LORD *hath done great things for us; whereof we are glad. Turn again our captivity, O* LORD, *as the streams in the south. They that sow in tears shall reap in joy. He that goeth forth and weepeth, bearing precious seed, shall doubtless come again with rejoicing, bringing his sheaves with him.* Psalm 126:1-6

CHAPTER 26

LEARNING IN A VARIETY OF WAYS

A wise man will hear, and will increase learning; and a man of understanding shall attain unto wise counsels. Proverbs 1:5

Today is the first day of school for children all over the state of Florida. It is a sad day for many students, but an exciting day for others. Starting fresh in a new school year is like wiping the slate clean and beginning again. Learning new information is easy for some and very difficult and frustrating for others. There are a variety of methods to learning which include visual, auditory, and hands-on. Using all three methods together make it easier for most people to learn faster.

I have taught at a Christian school and have also home schooled my three sons. Teachers learn so much from their students about how to teach. A method of teaching that works well on one student does not always work well on other students. Some students have trouble memorizing. I decided to add a song to our daily practice of memorizing the bones in the body in my science class. The Junior High students loved the song and participated excitedly. One of the most fulfilling achievements as a teacher was when my students were able to memorize the bones of the body by singing the song we learned together. Music allows both halves of the brain to be used; thereby, making it easier for all types of learners. Adding motions to the song, we also incorporated muscle memory learning. We were using our eyes, ears, and hands to memorize.

Learning comes from repetition. It is just a matter of how much repetition is required for different individuals. It may take one person just one time of seeing, hearing, or reading information to memorize it. Others, it may take twenty times. As teachers, it is important that we do not bore the ones who memorize rapidly. By making the learning fun, boredom does not become part of the equation. Games, music, motions, and hands-on experiences produce a classroom where everyone is able to learn at their own pace in a non-segregating setting.

It is important to teach the material that increases learning, then to reiterate what was taught in a fun game. If you want someone to learn, allow them to have fun while learning. Using stories (whether personal, historical, or creative) is another way to grab the attention of the students and assist in their learning process.

One of the most fun activities we would do in my science class was to work together during class time and build paper mache volcanoes. We started with wrapping the paper mache around a wire frame to shape it as a volcano. Each student would paint his own volcano to represent what he wanted to express. On the final day of the project, each student would bring a 2-liter Diet Coke and white Mentos candies. The chemical reaction between the Diet Coke and candy created a simulated volcanic eruption. We would take turns making our volcanoes erupt in the field with laughter and excitement. This hands-on approach to learning taught them how to paper mache. It allowed them to use wiring for shaping and to express themselves through their creative painting of their volcano. We also learned what happens chemically when white Mentos candies are dropped into a 2-liter Diet Coke. As we worked on the same part of the volcano each day assigned, students were able to walk around and see many different approaches to the same idea. We learned a little about each other's personalities from how they painted their volcano. It allowed the right-brained, artistic students who sometimes have difficulty memorizing to shine.

As a little girl, whenever my neighborhood friends asked me what I wanted to play, most of the time, I wanted to play school and be the teacher. I am a natural organizer and teaching demands organization skills. I like to find ways to help others learn. Hearing about a subject does not facilitate learning as well as if the subject is taken by the student with a hands-on approach added to the process. If you tell me ten times how to do a process on the computer, I still may not know how to do it. If you tell me and then have me do the same process a few times myself, I will learn it because I am physically doing it. This also applies to most children. Few are auditory learners, so by seeing and using a hands-on approach, it makes learning so much easier and fun for the child.

Every person, no matter the age, should always be learning. I want to keep my mind active by reading, memorizing, and exercising my brain. When young, the mind is like a sponge that absorbs quickly. As we age, more and more repetition is required. I had an exciting opportunity to act as a grandma in our church's Christmas play and cantata. I have been in a variety of plays over my lifetime. I have a newspaper clipping of myself acting in a play at my elementary school in fourth grade. I realize that at age 47, the repetition needed to memorize all of my lines was excessive. As our brains age, it takes longer to accomplish tasks, but it is achievable. Older people have a more fulfilling life when they are using their brain every day in some fashion or hobby. Taking an art class, learning a new language, playing words with friends, playing chess or checkers, or whatever they prefer are just a few great ways to keep your brain active and healthy. Learning should be a lifelong process that never stops.

Give instruction to a wise man, and he will be yet wiser: teach a just man, and he will increase in learning. The fear of the LORD is the beginning of wisdom: and the knowledge of the holy is understanding. Proverbs 9:9-10

CHAPTER 27

YOU CANNOT OUT GIVE GOD

Give, and it shall be given unto you; good measure, pressed down, and shaken together, and running over, shall men give into your bosom. For with the same measure that ye mete withal it shall be measured to you again. Luke 6:38

When God lays it on my heart to give, I like to joyfully give and then watch His hand at work in my life with all of the blessings He gives back to me. I don't give to get back; truly it is more blessed to give than to receive. I have heard it said that when you give, the brain releases a chemical equal to the release of a runner's endorphin. I believe this to be true. Giving to others brings so much joy to me that if I had to choose between only being able to give or to receive gifts, I would choose to give.

God laid it on the hearts of my husband and me to give to a family in need. Soon after giving, our family was asked to go out to eat with another family after church. They paid for our entire family's meal. It was such a blessing. It is impossible to out give God.

Our son has given above and beyond to two different churches that he attended while in college. He tithed at both churches and gave in many other ways above this also. God continues to give back to him. He decided to give a certain amount of money to thank God for His blessings. After that decision, God blessed him immediately by having two different people give him $100 this week. One of the people who gave to him was a pastor who understands the trials ahead of him at Bible College and the other was a missionary family that just happened to visit our church. It was the night our pastor and the men of the church prayed a dedication prayer for Jacob prior to his going to Bible College. The missionary had the gift of giving and he understands that he cannot out give God. His gift to Jacob was a huge financial blessing.

When we invest in the work of God and telling others about Jesus Christ and His Gospel that is the best way to ensure a return. God's Word does not return void. Whether we invest monetarily with money or volunteering with our time, when giving with a joyful heart, we are always blessed. I just packaged together a gift of clothes and "back to school" supplies for two needy children to encourage them in the Lord. I know God will bless that joyful giving. I am now seeking God in how I can give to someone else. I want the nudge of who and how much and what to give to come from God. There have been times that I could have given to someone, but the Lord put it on my heart not to give. It turned out that because I waited on the Lord, the need was taken care of in a better way. Wait on the Lord and He will give you the desires of your heart. When our heart is right, His desires become our desires.

My friend and I have agreed to hold each other accountable for different aspects of our lives. This week we both realized we were allowing anxiety to overcome our joy. We decided to have a "Hands Off" week. This means that we will pray specifically for our needs and cry out to God for help, but we cannot do anything to solve our problems in our own strength.

Her father had lost his job and she was very worried about necessities for their lives. Instead of having panic attacks and worrying herself sick, she decided to have a stress-free week and give it all to God. Three days later her dad got a job. In today's economy with the lack of available jobs, this is definitely a miracle and answer to our prayers. God's ways are so much better than our ways. I could take time to plan out and imagine how a problem could be solved, but when I trust God to take care of the situation for me, His ways are so much better than I can ever dream or imagine.

Our oldest son started Bible College in California. He attended a job fair because he needs a job to pay his way through college. I specifically prayed for a job paying at least $25/hr. with daytime hours after classes. I wanted it to be a job that he would immensely enjoy and have a passion for. I prayed for him to work at least 20-30 hours a week. As part of my hands off week, I cried out to God and reminded Him how faithful Jacob had been to serve Him and how much he loves Him. He could be such a great witness and light in the community there. I excitedly waited to see how God would far exceed my expectations. Jacob was blessed with a job in the community selling door to door. Even though he had a hurt knee and needed surgery, he was able to walk with no problems. God blessed him mightily this year with sales and earnings beyond our dreams. I enjoyed seeing the blessings of God fall generously from heaven. He recently accepted an internship position at Lancaster Baptist Church which is a true honor.

Over the past few months, I was able to give joyfully to those in need with my personal savings. I am on a journey to out give God, knowing that this is impossible. I recently gave $100 each to two young people who have devoted their lives to the work of the Lord and needed the money. God put it on my heart to do so. I also asked my three sons and husband to give along with me, which they did. I cried out to God because I saw another family in need that I wanted to give money to also. I prayed for God to give me money personally so I could give to those in need. Before He gave me money to pass on to this family, He solved the problem so the need no longer existed. This morning in my devotions, I was once again praying for money so I could give to others in need. God reminded me that He took care of that problem just from my prayers.

My husband and I love to give to our sons and our favorite way is by huge surprises. Our son Jacob was going to go to Bible College in California. His car was older than him and becoming more of a money pit than a help. We decided we would surprise him by giving him a car. He and my husband would drive it cross-country to California from Florida for a once in a lifetime father and son bonding trip. Our second son, Tim, had a car accident while driving his dad's Toyota Tundra. He was "t-boned" while pulling across a four-lane street. The driver's side door was crushed in all the way flush with his seat. If he had been driving our van, he would have probably been severely injured. I truly believe angels stood between him and the mangled metal. The good part of this tragedy was that our gas guzzling truck was classified as "totaled" by the insurance company and we were able to put the insurance money down on a gas efficient vehicle. The gas money for the small car is so much less compared to what we use to spend on our large truck.

Tim's accident was in November, so Andy and I enjoyed our new 2012 Honda Civic for several months until the next summer. When Jacob graduated from the University of Central Florida the summer of 2013, Andy and I surprised him with our 2012 Honda Civic to take to California. We actually bought a new 2013 Honda Civic for us because we love the type of car so much.

When tragedy happens, like a car wreck, so many times God is performing an unexpected miracle for us. We should immediately look for God's hand working in every tragedy we experience. Jeremiah 29:11 says, *"For I know the thoughts that I think toward you, saith the Lord, thoughts of peace, and not of evil, to give you an expected end."* God only wants His best for each of us. When we are facing trials, hardships, or tragedies, we need to look for ways to give God the glory and keep our eyes open for a miracle and blessing. Even if the only blessing is our growing closer spiritually to God through the experience, we should be thankful for each hardship placed in our lives.

These things I have spoken unto you, that in me ye might have peace. In the world ye shall have tribulation: but be of good cheer; I have overcome the world. John 16:33

CHAPTER 28

TRUSTING GOD TO ANSWER PRAYERS

When thou saidst, Seek ye my face; my heart said unto thee, Thy face, LORD, will I seek. Psalm 27:8

A feeling of overwhelming frustration and fear swallows me up as I hear something I never want to hear again. I am driving my van on the way to the community college to pick up books for my son's two classes. I was hoping the books he had from his older brother would still be used. To my frustration and dismay, they were not. As I drive to the college bookstore, I am called with extremely depressing news. I want to yell, cry, and tell someone off. The tears do not come, but the storm cloud of burden over my soul is now my companion. I try to push it away, but it is like pushing away fog; it just stays there.

A phone call is made to confirm and I am told even more overwhelmingly disappointing news. I cannot believe this has happened again. I go into the bookstore in a daze. The line to get the needed books is about twenty people long. I drudgingly go to the back of the line and stand there with my foggy mind. I have another phone call while standing there and seem to become more and more discouraged. Finally my turn arrives. Praise the Lord, they have the needed books. I now move into one of the two lines for the register which snakes completely across the store. The books are heavy and I have not eaten yet. I start to feel light headed like I could faint at any moment. I find a place to set my books down and move them along with me as I step. Finally another cashier opens up and my line becomes two lines. I quickly move to the front of my line and wait for about five more people ahead of me.

As I am moving along in the line, I am being texted with how frustrated another person is about the news. As I settle him down and ask him to stop being worried and be a prayer warrior, I am holding back tears in this very public place. I ask him to pray for me that I don't burst out crying in front of everyone. I get a text from my youngest son at this time saying that he got the job he was interviewing for at McDonald's - Yippee - good news. I needed that shot in the arm of joy and happiness. "I am so excited and happy for you. You have wanted a job for so long and now you have one. Congratulations!" Pulling encouragement from a saddened soul was difficult but I did it because he was experiencing a new stage in his life and I wanted to be a happy encouragement at that moment of time for him.

Finishing my transaction for $400 worth of books, I head out the door. I quickly walk back to the van to return a call to my husband and he and I talk about the situation. It seems so dark and cloudy and I was afraid it would be this way for months on end. I still have errands to run, so I stop by Wal-Mart on the way home.

The person that I need to talk to about the situation is away, so several hours pass before I see him. God gave me time to vent to my husband and talk to God in my mind. As I finally am able to talk to the person who is experiencing the situation, God has settled my heart and given me wisdom. God has gone ahead of me and taken care of it with giving the person wisdom of how to handle the situation. We decide to follow through with this way of dealing with it and feel at peace.

My heart was so upset, but I went to God knowing that He already knows everything and would handle it for me. Thinking it would take months or a whole year of torture to walk through the trial of muck and slime, I was happily encouraged by God's way of going before me. Instead of reacting and trying to control it myself, I knew that I must seek God's face and trust Him. I have been faithful to him in prayer about this situation for years and I know He will bless us with His best for my pursuit for God's will in this area. There have been many days that I have cried out to God over situations in our sons' lives that I have been praying about since they were babies. I claimed the Scriptures' promises that the effectual and fervent prayer of a righteous man availeth much. I trust God to answer my prayers.

Whatever you are going through that has your heart so heavy that you physically ache, know that Jesus has been there and understands how you feel. You cannot eat because you are emotionally drained. You cannot concentrate because your mind is overtaken with what seems like an impossible situation. By no fault of your own, your world is crumbling all around you. Maybe because of your own self-centered decisions and mistakes, everything is falling apart, go to God. He will be there for you.

He promises that if we seek Him, we will find Him. It has to be a sincere desire to know God personally and accept Jesus as your Savior. Believing that Jesus died on the cross for the sins of the world and rose again three days later is the only way to salvation. We are all sinners and need the perfect sacrifice of Jesus Christ in order to go to heaven. Once you are a Christian, then God will hear your prayers. We, as Christians, must ask forgiveness for our daily sins, so our prayers may also be heard. God's desire is to help His people through the good and bad times in our lives. We must reach out to Him. He is waiting for you only to ask.

And thou, Solomon my son, know thou the God of thy father, and serve him with a perfect heart and with a willing mind: for the LORD searcheth all hearts, and understandeth all the imaginations of the thoughts: if thou seek him, he will be found of thee; but if thou forsake him, he will cast thee off forever. 1 Chronicles 28:9

CHAPTER 29

AND…THERE HE GOES

Cast thy burden upon the LORD, and he shall sustain thee: he shall never suffer the righteous to be moved. Psalm 55:22

Today starts a new phase of my life. My oldest son is driving to Lancaster, California from Cocoa, Florida to attend West Coast Baptist College for pastoral studies. He and his dad are on a 41-hour 14-minute cross-country drive of 2,723 miles.

They will make eight stops before arriving at their destination. The first stop is at the home of Jacob's Nana and Papa in Jacksonville, Florida. Tomorrow Jacob will be teaching his Papa's Sunday school class of over 100 saints who love our family dearly. I know he will have many prayer warriors there keeping him on their minds and in their prayers as he heads to Bible College.

He graduated August, 2013 from the University of Central Florida in Orlando, Florida where he lived in a dorm for the past two years. I was accustomed to him not being home all the time; he would come home some weekends and I could always travel the 45-minute drive to see him at any time. He moved out of his dorm in July when his classes were finished and has lived at home the last few weeks. We have enjoyed this special time of being together.

Our family went to Sonny's BBQ for our last family meal together before their trip to California officially began. I laughed and was being a bit silly knowing that in a few minutes my son would be driving off into manhood and starting life on his own. I took way too many pictures to the point that Jacob said, "Mom, it's not like I'm dying." No, he was not dying, but something inside of me was dying. He has become a man and now only needs his parents as an adult would, not as a child.

My husband and I have been successful in rearing Jacob to being independent and leaving the nest. This has been our goal all along. I want my sons to be independent, strong, ethical, godly men who stand on their own two feet with God at their side. I want them to have godly character to make good decisions to please Jesus and give Him glory. I did not rear them to be perfect, because no one is perfect. I do want them to admit their mistakes, ask for forgiveness, and learn from them. God gives us new mercies every morning. He does not expect perfection because He knows how frail we are. He does expect us to ask forgiveness for our sins and do our best to be like His Son, Jesus.

It is of the LORD's mercies that we are not consumed, because his compassions fail not. They are new every morning: great is thy faithfulness. Lamentations 3:22-23

After our dinner was complete, we walked outside to our cars. I hugged him goodbye and he held on to me extra-long. It was as if he realized that he was spreading his wings and flying into manhood. He knows this hug must last him for a prolonged period of time. I did not cry when I said goodbye, but I am crying now.

Having my firstborn leave home is harder than I thought it would be; I feel like part of my heart has been torn off and it aches so much. I know he will always be part of our lives, just in a different way now. Arriving back home, when I walked into the house, I saw a hand towel that has a B on it to represent our last name, Bundy. I bought this for Jacob when he moved to the UCF dorm. I turned and walked away to not be reminded of him. I wanted to take the hand towel to the bathroom in our bedroom, but could not. The pain of the reminder was too much at that moment.

For Jacob's UCF graduation, I had a mouse pad made with 14 of my favorite pictures of him on it. I gave one to his dad for his office at work and the other one I gave to Jacob. He left it here, so I have it by our computer in our bedroom enjoying it. It is funny how I have a hard time looking at a hand towel, but I'm enjoying reminiscing over his pictures: a baby picture of him smiling; a kindergarten graduation picture; a third-grade picture of him holding his Bible that he just completed reading for the first time; a picture of him on Hadrian's Wall in England; a picture of him as an eighth grader dressed up as the Bible character Levi for the play "Joseph, God Meant It for Good"; his Vipers' football picture in uniform and another Senior picture of him in his football jersey standing by the goal post that looks like a cross; he and his brothers dressed up as cowboys for Roundup day at church with guns pulled on each other; he and his brothers in Mexico when they went snorkeling in the Gulf of Mexico; a picture of Jacob and his brother Tim on the cruise ship all dressed up in suits for formal night; a senior picture at his college campus in a suit; his college graduation picture in cap and gown; a picture of him in the pulpit at church; and last but not least, a picture of him standing in front of the Space Shuttle Orbiter Endeavor, which was secured on top of a 747 airplane on its final flight to its new home in California. This mouse pad is like a walk down memory lane to wonderful reminders of Jacob's life.

Starting this "empty nesting" made me wonder how I would react. I cry tears of happiness and joy because I am so proud of the past 19 years of work to help him become successful and independent. My brain does not listen to my heart when it says it is okay and it is not a big deal that my firstborn is leaving home as a man. Being so excited about his future, I just cannot wait to see how The Lord will use his life. Questions roll into my mind wondering who he will marry, where he will work during his college years, what he will do, and where he will live when he graduates. Knowing God will take care of him, I release him and God says to me, "Well done, you have been my faithful steward of my child, Jacob. Now you may enjoy the benefits of your labor."

Walking around this morning, I have a heavy heart. I want the pain and sadness to be over so I can go on without thinking about our son being gone from our home. I feel like I need a really good cry but it will not come. I tear up while watching a movie and know it is because I am emotional with my empty nesting syndrome. I stay busy and keep my mind occupied. The next morning, Jacob is lined up to teach his Papa's Sunday school class. He has prepared and is ready. This is an awesome first opportunity for Jacob to speak to senior adults. He is feeling a bit intimidated and even blanks out on his introduction. His preparation work allows him to carry on and do a fantastic job. I am at my own church this Sunday and a bit sad that I am missing him speak. Andy took pictures and sent them to me and this encourages me.

Sunday night I teach a discipleship class which I really enjoy. Tonight is extra hard for me because I have a heavy heart. I have prayed often for God to give me peace to soothe my heavy heart. As I teach and we pray for each other in tears and encourage each other with words, my spirit is lifted. Hearing God's Word always encourages and heals my broken heart. My younger two sons went to church out of town with friends who are leaving for the same college as Jacob. The boys were gone the whole day which made me feel a bit lonely. I actually embraced the alone time and enjoyed the peace and quiet because I do not get it that often. Unfortunately, I did not sleep well. My mind was busy and would not rest.

With my two younger sons back home, I am feeling much more comforted. They need me and I am glad to be here for them. This is their senior year in high school. They are taking all of their classes at the community college this year except a couple electives. I have decided I still do not want to work this year because I want to be available as a support, encouragement, and help to them. I am taking this year to write this book that I have always wanted to write. God is so good to give us our heart's desire when it coincides with His will.

After only a few days, God has comforted my heart and the sadness has changed to excitement about Jacob's future. The distraction of home schooling and writing my book has kept me busy and focused. I was wondering how long my heart would ache so badly. I know it will be harder when all three of my sons leave. For now, I am resting in the arms of God and learning from Him. With God, I am never alone even if no one is around.

I have no greater joy than to hear that my children walk in truth. 3 John 4
For he hath said, I will never leave thee, nor forsake thee. Hebrews 13:5b

CHAPTER 30

FEELING YOUNG WITH FRIENDS

A man that hath friends must shew himself friendly: and there is a friend that sticketh closer than a brother. Proverbs 18:24

Sitting at a table of ladies who are in their forties in age, we reminisce about how life was when we were teenagers. I was amazed that all of us used to roller skate. Memories of how I would skate with all of my high school friends flooded back into my mind, and I felt 16 years old again. Going down memory lane has a way of making you feel young again.

Tonight at our ladies' meeting at church, the theme was a carnival. I walked in the doorway and saw the artistic display of the food carnival style. There were game booths set up all around the room. I froze because I thought that I had mixed up the time and date of the ladies meeting and walked into a children's church activity. I looked around and saw only ladies and someone assured me it was the right place and time.

It is funny how a carnival themed meeting can make a 46-year old woman feel like a child. After we ate our hotdogs and popcorn with soda, it was time for the games. If you won the game, then you were awarded a prize. I tried the dart game, but only hit two out of the three balloons that were needed to win. I move on to the ring bottle toss game. You only needed to hit one bottle to win. After three tries, I hit my target head on and yelled, "Yippee, I won" as I ran to the prize table. I looked at the possible prizes and picked up a cool looking vegetable chopper. I held it and continued to eyeball the other prizes on the table. My eyes met a beautiful pink object. I picked it up and opened it to see what it was. It was a "Thirty-One" notebook organizer with pad, Velcro sleeve big enough for a kindle and a small pocket to hold a cell phone. I put down the vegetable slicer and took the pink organizer that was exactly the kind of item that I love.

God is so good to give us what we really need when we need it. I had carried my car keys, phone, and a pen into the meeting. As I was about to get into my car, I almost went back inside the house to grab a small bag to keep them in for the meeting. I decided against it and drove on. After I won the pink organizer, I sat back down feeling happy and organized as I put my cell phone in the cell phone holder along with my pen and my keys into the Velcro pocket feeling happy and organized. I was glad that I had not gone back into the house to grab a bag to hold my things because God had provided for me exactly when and what I needed.

I am trusting the Lord this week with a huge need and am waiting on His perfect timing. I know He will provide according to His riches in glory. He promises to take care of us and our needs. I will be faithful to do my part and then wait on the Lord to do His part. No matter how much we give to Him, we cannot out give God. I have put that to the test many times. This past week, I received a gift card to a store and was able to buy a desk chair for my bedroom plus many other items. I won a perfect item for me, the pink organizer. I receive joy out of giving to others, but God also gives back to me in so many different, unusual ways.

Our youngest son Caleb began his first job tonight. He has wanted a job since he was 14. As I dropped him off for orientation, it brought back memories of my first job at a department store. I was 15 when I filled out many applications. They did not want to hire me because of my young age. I was a senior in high school and really wanted a job to save for college. One day, I went to the small cafeteria in the store and filled out an application again. As I was sitting there, the store manager saw me and was impressed by my persistence, so he finally gave me the job. I worked hard and was promoted from cashier to Department Head of the Photography Department. I became one of their best employees. The manager took a chance of hiring someone so young, but it ended up being a smart decision for him.

As Caleb begins his first job, he is so excited to now be able to save for college. He was telling me how he would tithe, give to missions, have a little spending money and then save $100 per week for college. I am so proud of him and know he will do great.

It has been said, "You are as young as you feel." There is much truth to this. As my body is aging and has aches and pains due to wear and tear, my mind and spirit are still that of a 16-year old girl from years ago. It may be harder for me to accomplish tasks the way I did as a teenager, but I can still accomplish them. I am portraying a grandma in a play at my church for the Christmas cantata. I have been in many plays over the years starting when I was in fourth grade. I took on this grandma role determined that I would memorize every line and also add emotion to the character so the name of Jesus Christ would be honored and glorified. As part of the play, I lead my granddaughter to Jesus as her personal Savior. My prayers for months have been that many souls would come to know Jesus as their Savior through this play. I knew it would be much harder for me to memorize the part, but with hours upon hours of practice and repetition, God will be glorified and I will see one day in heaven how many souls received Jesus as their Savior. Feeling old? Change your thoughts to positive ones of what you can do at the age you are now and be a help and encouragement to others. This always brings joy back to yourself.

And whatsoever ye do, do it heartily, as to the Lord, and not unto men.
Colossians 3:23

CHAPTER 31

SEEING TRUTH

Wherefore putting away lying, speak every man truth with his neighbour.
Ephesians 4:25a

Truth has a way of ringing with clarity. If it doesn't sound right and fit, it's probably a lie. People are subtle and use tricky words to tell a lie as they manipulate others. Some young ladies will tell stories to get sympathy from naïve young men. They look for what the boy is sensitive about and then they will use sad stories to provoke a protector spirit from them or to get them to do what they want.

My prayer for my family is that we are able to see through lies and manipulation and not be controlled by it. The problem with lies is that it becomes a monster that will literally eat you alive. You may tell a lie and then you must tell another to cover it. You then may forget one of the lies so you have to lie again. If you tell the truth, you will not have to remember anything because it is the truth and the story will always be the same.

People who lie have a huge character flaw and others lose trust in them. In court, if you tell one lie, nothing else you say is considered truthful. If a person lies, it also says something about who he is. It says he is willing to risk friendship and trust to manipulate and get what he wants. It says that this person cannot be trusted without reservation. Renewed trust takes a very long time and just one lie takes you back to ground zero again. Compulsive liars are very self-centered because they care about what they want for themselves more than any other person at that time.

What does it take to stop this character flaw and become trustworthy again? It takes determining in your heart that you will not lie again for any reason. It also takes thinking before you speak. Count to ten and think about if the answer is the truth or a lie in any way. You have to be completely dedicated to not lying again. If you mess up and lie, you need to immediately tell the person it is a lie and tell the truth instead. This is a humbling task, but a great way to rebuild trust and character.

You should also have an accountability partner to talk to daily and be questioned by about the lies you have told and how you made them right. You must see lying as sin and not just a white lie that doesn't hurt anyone. You must be dedicated to stay on task and be consistent to stop lying. For habitual liars and manipulators, it is a natural response to lie. You must replace the habit with a new learned response of telling the absolute truth.

Everyone lies and everyone must work daily at telling the truth. We are all faced with opportunities throughout the day to lie. Many times, a person's goal is to make himself look good, felt sorry for, or special in the eyes of others, so he can feel better about himself. The irony with this way of thinking is that when lies are exposed, the person looks ridiculous and becomes untrustworthy to everyone. Instead of making himself look good, he has made himself seen as a person that cannot be trusted.

If you are in a situation where you feel trapped and unable to tell the truth, the best action is to go to your parents or other authority figure and seek their help instead of living with the sin and lie. Every Christian has times where they make mistakes and sin. We can benefit from our mistakes if we learn from them and never do them again.

If a person cannot be trusted to tell the truth, the person cannot be depended upon. He cannot be a person of character until he admits his wrong doing and works to overcome this habitual sin. It doesn't matter how "spiritual" he or she is; continual, compulsive lying is a character flaw that reaches into every aspect of who the person is. Speak the truth, think before you speak, and rebuild trust over time. These guidelines will help build back your character and trustworthiness.

Stand therefore, having your loins girt about with truth, and having on the breastplate of righteousness. Ephesians 6:14

CHAPTER 32

BACK IN THE SADDLE AGAIN

Know ye not that ye are the temple of God, and that the Spirit of God dwelleth in you?
1 Corinthians 3:16

Here I am back at it again losing the weight I gained on vacation. It has taken me two months to lose the weight I gained in one week on vacation. Now that I am 47 years old, it takes a small miracle to lose weight. I exercise by walking at least two miles 5-6 times a week which takes me about 40 minutes or I bike five miles which takes me about 30 minutes. I am eating less and much healthier.

As one who has lost and gained many pounds over the past several years, I am not trying to give any advice. I guess it all started with having babies. I gained and did not work hard enough to lose it before I was pregnant again twelve months later. Having two active sons should have worked the weight off of me easily; but I ended up pregnant again nine months later as a surprise.

Our sons are now twenty, eighteen, and seventeen, and yet I feel like I still have some weight I need to lose and keep off. I did lose down to a healthy weight when my sons were about ten, nine, and seven. I don't even know how all of a sudden I seemed to gain back weight and even more pounds than I had before. On July 1, 2013, I decided I was tired of being slothful about it and started to take action. Two months later, I had lost eleven pounds and 4 ½ inches. Today is April 1, 2014 and I have lost over twenty pounds and am maintaining. My bike rides are helping me build up muscle and lose fat. I feel fantastic and give all the glory to God. Only

God can help me stay focused and not get distracted by temporary pleasures. I don't care what the food is and how yummy it looks, it is not worth the pain that I will have to go through to work it off.

My youngest son, Caleb, has started weight lifting and running to get healthy and lose weight. He is also eating less. He has lost seventeen pounds over the last eight months as he lost fat and gained muscle. He was made fun of as a child since he was nine years old. I look back at pictures of him and do not see a fat or even chubby child, I see a boy with large leg muscles and a broad chest. Many of the boys in his class were very skinny with tiny muscles and they saw his large muscles as fat. It breaks my heart to see any child made fun of for any reason. I had a speech problem when I was young and had trouble pronouncing certain sounds. I remember to this day a girl making fun of the way I spoke. My heart's desire is to become a speaker for ladies' retreats and conferences. Overcoming my speech problem and being able to be a speaker to encourage ladies would be one of my greatest accomplishments in life. I am praying for God to open doors in that direction in His timing.

Several of my friends and I were encouragers to each other in the past as we met once a week to weigh and support each other. Keeping each other accountable by telling if we lost, gained, or stayed the same was an inspiring motivator. The person in charge of the meeting moved and we did not continue the meetings. Each of us gained back some if not all of our weight. Being accountable to someone requires you to work harder because you have to face up to the truth of losing or not in front of others. It also helps because it inspires a competitive spirit among most people.

It is strange how sometimes those closest to you can influence you to fail the easiest. I am determined not to have sugar because of how it negatively affects my health. My family knows this and I have asked that no sugar food or drinks be brought into the house. If someone brings home cupcakes or donuts, I take them after they have eaten what they want and throw them in the trash so they cannot be taken back out. I do not want to be tempted, so I do not want sweets in the house.

Another huge temptation is sweet tea. My husband and sons love sweet tea. I have to be alert and not habitually pick it up and drink some. I usually drink water and occasionally will drink 100% fruit juice. The sugar in drinks, except 100% fruit juice, causes my muscles to ache like I have the flu, so I have learned it is not worth drinking.

Exercise is so very important for your physical and mental health. I walk and bike for several good reasons: health, strong heart; strong bones; balance and muscle strength; a positive mental outlook; prayer warrior time; opportunities to tell others about Jesus and invite them to church; seeing God's beautiful creation; tell God how much I love Him and how amazing He is; to think through problems in my life. This helps me to be more joyful, be at peace, relax, sleep better, feel better, and to be easier to live with. Exercise is a great medicine for many issues whether physical or mental. Endorphins are released which actually make you feel better.

Being healthy is a great goal for everyone. Eating healthy and exercising is a great way to make oneself the best physically and mentally he or she can be. Having someone to hold you accountable for what you lose or gain will actually encourage and challenge you much more. Seek God about what is right for your body type and weight. A weight that is right for my height and body shape is not right for someone much taller or shorter than me. It is not about a number as much as it is about looking and feeling your best so you can be used for the glory and service of Jesus.

Beloved, I wish above all things that thou mayest prosper and be in health, even as thy soul prospereth. 3 John 2

CHAPTER 33

DEPENDING UPON GOD, NOT PEOPLE

Come unto me, all ye that labour and are heavy laden, and I will give you rest.
Matthew 11:28

Why do we run to people with our problems, heartaches, and loneliness instead of going to the One who created us? God knows every detail of each situation we are in and He knows exactly how we feel. He sent His Son Jesus to the earth for the purpose of dying for the sins of everyone. He knows loss, pain, heartache, and loneliness more deeply than we can ever imagine.

We do not trust God to understand or handle our problems for us, so we talk to people instead and expect their trivial experiences in life to be helpful to us. It is like comparing a sand castle that is made by a child to the whole Grand Canyon. There is no comparison; yet we continue to look at that sand castle just knowing somehow it will help us.

God is right beside us desiring us to come to Him instead of other people. He has tears in His eyes because we snub our noses at Him and push Him aside so we can run over to someone who is not even a Christian for comfort with your problems. It hurts Him so badly, yet He continues to love us and is there waiting for us to ask for His help.

The problem with continually running to people, especially those who are not Christians for comfort is that we are missing out on spiritual growth and blessings from God. We tie God's hands so He cannot bless us to His fullest because we are not trusting in Him. We tell ourselves that we are being helped by people by their encouragement when in actuality we are becoming codependent upon them instead of completely dependent upon God.

God wants to be part of all of our heartaches, sad moments, and disappointments. He is a jealous God and does not want to share us with anyone. Instead of spending time in prayer crying out to God with our problems, we spend our time texting people who may or may not be in God's will to give us advice. If we text someone who is not saved and talk about our problems with them, we are going to a carnal, worldly person for advice. Even if we do not officially inquire for advice, we are asking by telling them our problems. They feel they need to encourage us and give us helpful words. So in essence, we are going to someone who is against our Savior, Jesus Christ for help.

Our first reaction to any problem or dilemma in our lives should be to cry out to God in prayer for help and wisdom. We will not get Godly wisdom from the world. The Bible says in Matthew 6:33, "*Seek ye first the kingdom of God, and His righteousness; and all these things shall be added unto you.*" Our minds and hearts should be on the things of God and He will take care of our problems and needs.

Matthew 10:29-31 says, "*Are not two sparrows sold for a farthing? And one of them shall not fall on the ground without your Father. But the very hairs of your head are all numbered. Fear ye not therefore, ye are of more value than many sparrows.*" Our heavenly Father knows every detail about every part of our lives. He cares about us to the point that He knows every hair upon our heads.

Is it not ironic that we refuse to truly trust the One who cares the most about what happens to us? People come and go and many don't really care if we are in or out of their lives; God is here to stay and will never leave nor forsake us. Hebrews 13:5 says, "*Let your conversation be without covetousness; and be content with such things as ye have; for He hath said, I will never leave thee, nor forsake thee*". It is as though we have inherited millions of dollars, but we believe we are better off refusing our inheritance and working a job that pays minimum wage.

May our eyes be opened to our God and how much He wants to be part of every aspect of our lives. May we trust Him to take care of our every need and not seek others to do it for us. True faith is built when we go to God and see Him overcome our problems again and again. What kind of a life do we want to live? Do we want a faith that wavers so much that we invariably run to people or do we want to have a faith so strong in God that it is natural to run to Him constantly and consistently? Our faith and to whom we go to will determine what kind of life we will have.

And The Lord said, If ye had faith as a grain of mustard seed, ye might say unto this sycamore tree, Be thou plucked up by the root, and be thou planted in the sea; and it should obey you. Luke 17:6

CHAPTER 34

SUGAR IS MY ENEMY

There hath no temptation taken you but such as is common to man: but God is faithful, who will not suffer you to be tempted above that ye are able; but will with the temptation also make a way to escape, that ye may be able to bear it. 1 Corinthians 10:13

It is 12:20 A.M. and I cannot sleep due to aches and pains throughout my whole body. I took some ibuprofen and it has not started to help yet. I know I am aching because I have not had sugar for months and tonight I had a dessert with my meal. For years now, I have known that sugar causes my body to ache all over like the flu and gives me a headache. It is ironic how I can know this and forget it also.

My motto is "no sugar because it is not worth the pain it causes." I forget how extreme the pain is when I don't eat sugar because I go for so long without it and don't feel the aches it causes. I pray before I go to friends' houses for dinner or to restaurants that I will not eat sugar. Tonight, I fell into a nicely hidden trap. Our son Jacob won a $100 gift certificate to an upscale restaurant for leading his team to win the UCF Business Cornerstone Competition. As a gesture of thanking us as his parents for all we have done for him in his life and education, he gave us this wonderful dining experience.

Before we arrived at the restaurant, I prayed that I would not eat sugar. My husband and I sat down and we decided to order the more reasonably priced meals which included a main course, a side, and dessert. I decided I would give my dessert to my husband or take it home to my sons. The waiter explained the dessert to us: a sampling of cheesecake, a chocolate and walnut cookie, and a rhubarb jelly for dipping the cookie in. My mind started thinking about the dessert and how our dinner represented our firstborn son taking flight as an adult on his own. I decided to celebrate by eating the dessert myself. I have found that it is often the silliest reasons or perhaps the most emotional reasons that put us in hidden pits looking up into the sky above wondering how we got there.

About thirty minutes after we left the restaurant, I started getting a headache and my brain felt foggy and sleepy. When we arrived home, I tried to sleep, but every pain receptor in my body seemed to be screaming out, "Why did you eat sugar? You know what it does to us!" I was aching from top of my head down to my toes. The ache in my knee I have had the last few days intensified to where I wanted to cry. Right then, I decided I don't care what emotional phase I am going through, I don't want to eat sugar ever again.

I have a friend who holds me accountable for not eating sugar and I hold her accountable also. I will have to tell her about my failure of eating sugar in the morning. At least I am being reminded of why I don't eat sugar and learning from my mistake.

The devil knows each of our shortcomings and how to trip us up. We think we are being so careful and even praying about it; but then all of a sudden it seems like we have been hit between the eyes by a big semi-truck and all we can do is stand there dumbfounded in unbelief. How do we keep from being tricked? I thought I had covered all of my bases by preparing myself for spiritual warfare against sugar. I have an accountability partner. I pray about it before I go into places where I know there will be temptation. I thought I was strong enough in my mind not to eat sugar; but perhaps I allowed the emotion of what the dinner represented to me to change my mind, I told myself it was ok this certain time to make it an exception. There is now a "no exception" rule for any reason added to my guidelines.

Now, I jump right back on that horse of no sugar, with no exceptions and plan to ride it through the rest of my life. I will be happy about it because I will not have muscle aches or headaches from this toxin in my body. I will talk to my accountability partner and tell her how I was led astray and how I will not let this happen again. Like the pain of childbirth fades away, I forget how absolutely agonizing these aches feel. It is as though I am being tormented in my body with excruciating aches that will not stop. My muscles feel as though they have been beaten by a meat tenderizer. My pain receptors are all firing and screaming out at the same time and the only person I can blame is me.

Praying, I beg God for forgiveness for eating something that I know causes my body harm. I ask Him to not let me forget the pain that is caused by sugar so I will not eat or drink it again. Life goes on and so do I with my mind made up - no exceptions. No matter how many people make special desserts for me or buy me something with sugar in it, I must say "no" for the sake and benefit of my health and spirituality.

What? know ye not that your body is the temple of the Holy Ghost which is in you, which ye have of God, and ye are not your own? For ye are bought with a price: therefore glorify God in your body, and in your spirit, which are God's. 1 Corinthians 6:19-20

CHAPTER 35

LET THE HANDS OFF BEGIN

Trust in the LORD with all thine heart; and lean not unto thine own understanding. In all thy ways acknowledge him, and he shall direct thy paths. Proverbs 3:5-6

Our firstborn son Jacob has been a Bible college student for less than a week and I am being taught that hands off and in God's Hands is the best place for him to be. Jacob graduated this summer, 2013 from UCF at 19 years of age. He was home schooled and was dual enrolled at the local community college during his high school years. He had also skipped 7th grade. He lived at UCF in the Honors College dorm when he was 17 and was also on the UCF Knight's football team. God has blessed him in so many ways and the past two years at UCF have been helpful in growing him spiritually. He worked as a sports intern at one church and volunteered as the youth leader at another church nearby. Jacob was asked, "How did you stay right with God while attending a secular college?" He answered, "I choose to stay busy in the work of the Lord by witnessing to college students, working with children and sports, and by teaching the teens about Jesus, my Savior."

He was only a 45-minute drive from home if there was an emergency or need. If his car broke down, his laptop was not working, or he locked his keys in his car, we were close enough to drive over to help him out. We received a phone call that his brand new laptop had stopped working, so we made sure he had a copy of the receipt so he could mail the laptop to the manufacturer for repairs. In the meantime while his new laptop was being repaired, my husband had someone check-out Jacob's old laptop so it could be used while he was waiting on his new one.

Last night at 12:30 am, my husband answers the phone. I was asleep and then awaken to the words "Jacob" and "emergency." In the fogginess of my sleep, my first thought is that Jacob is in emergency surgery and how quickly can I fly to be with him in the hospital. After waking up completely and talking to Jacob directly, I realize he hurt his knee playing football and he thought it would be alright. He just wanted to talk to me about it because I am a nurse. I was told that the knee was able to be moved around and popped back into place. I feel that he should be alright, but told him to let someone in leadership know about what happened so he can get help in the morning with crutches and a leg brace or compression bandage. We hung up and his father and I prayed quite a bit as we gave it to God and went back to sleep.

The next morning, I read what Jacob had written on his face book page: "So tonight for the intramural flag football combine out here at West Coast Baptist College I was playing running back in a drill, made a sharp cut to the right to shake one linebacker and then another to the left to shake the other one. On that second cut my knee buckled and gave out. I went to the ground in immense pain and couldn't move it. As I laid there on the ground, all I could think about was how much I had just lost: I wouldn't be able to walk for months; I wouldn't be able to get in and out of classes without great difficulty anymore; I wouldn't be able to drive; I wouldn't be able to play sports, do any work, or even stand in a pulpit to preach. I was scared to death.....I was terrified that I had just lost everything I took for granted. But thank God He had other plans for me. After a while on the ground, somebody started moving my knee around, and finally I was able to move it on my own in all directions. I still couldn't put a whole lot of pressure on it, but I was able to walk off the field with some assistance and get back to my dorm. Furthermore, the knee did not pop when it buckled. My knee is going to be real sore the next few days, but it should be fine...no permanent damage. It is funny how God teaches us thankfulness. In those minutes when I was on the ground, and I thought my ACL was torn or my knee popped out of place, and that my world had been flipped upside down, all of a sudden those routine things like being able to walk and work and stand in a pulpit, those things that I usually take for granted became a whole lot more important. Don't take the little, routine things for granted. Thank God for them every day because in the blink of an eye you could lose them on any day. Also please keep my knee in your prayers. It is going to be sore in the morning."

I was very pleased to see the amazing amount of learning Jacob had already experienced in less than a week of Bible College. I know his faith will grow mightily over the next three years. His first lesson was to trust God with his laptop and not stress about it because his classes start Monday and he is without a laptop. His second lesson was thankfulness and not taking anything for granted. I believe God is teaching him to slow down and be patient for his third lesson. I hope he learns it quickly.

My husband and I received a follow-up phone call from Jacob, but what we heard was totally unexpected. Jacob had called us back to talk with us about his knee diagnosis after seeing an orthopedic surgeon and having an MRI. He was on the UCF college football team and never injured, so we did not think this would be anything major.

He read the MRI findings sheet before he walked in to see his Orthopedic Surgeon. He texted us first, "About to meet the doc. I'm looking at the preliminary report…..it's bad….." He then sent us an image of the report on our phones. Andy was driving, so I read the report to him. Words that made me catch my breath were "ACL tear, bone injuries, fracture, and sprain." As soon as we saw ACL tear, we knew he would need to have surgery to repair the damage.

We comforted Jacob with words that whatever was needed, we would be there for him. If he needed surgery right away, I would fly to California and stay there as long as I was needed. We encouraged him to shine for God while he was going through this valley and to thank God for this hard time knowing he would draw closer to Him. His dad, as a wise father would do, encouraged him with scripture and song, "In everything give thanks, for this is the will of God in Christ Jesus. Can we praise God in the valley? There is a great song that a friend of mine sang in the past called, In the valley, He restores my soul." "When I'm low in spirit I cry Lord lift me up, I want to go higher with Thee. But nothing grows high on a mountain so He picked out a valley for me. And He leads me beside still waters somewhere in the valley below. And He draws me aside to be tested and tried, in the valley He restoreth my soul. It's dark as a dungeon and the sun seldom shines and I question the Lord why must this be? Then He tells me there's strength in my sorrow and there's victory in trials for me. Then He leads me beside the still waters. Down in the valley, He restoreth my soul."

Jacob asked us to pray for him because he thought it was going to be bad, but not this bad. He then saw the specialist who confirmed what we already knew would happen. He had to have ACL reconstructive surgery, but he could wait until he returned home in December.

Anyone who knows Jacob, knows he loves playing sports. He loves God most of all with all of his heart, then his favorite thing is sports. The doctor told him no sports for a year. He will have surgery and then six to nine months of physical therapy. He could walk and even jog, but no sports that would make his knee go side to side. God took something precious to Jacob and said "I want all of your focus on Me right now; I will give you back sports, but now it is all about Me".

His dad gave him some positive feedback, "It's not that bad son, and you can keep your job, walk and even jog. This does not affect your ability to learn and retain your schooling. This just serves to laser focus you this first year of school. Know that our God is with you every step of the way. Be willing to lean on Him. He is teaching you to depend on Him. You will need that in your ministry."

I also encouraged him by reminding him of a high school play titled: God knows better than I. "God is taking something very precious to you away for a year and then will return it. Joseph had many hard situations where he did his best and shined no matter where he was. Shine brightly son. People are watching."

Andy asked Jacob, "Why does a sovereign God allow bad things to happen to good people like you? He is forming in you the character you need to fulfill the assignment He has given you in life." Jacob replied, "Bad things happen to good people to make good people into better people."

Jacob can breathe, so He can continue to tell others about Jesus. He can walk, so he can go soul winning. He has a brain that is intact, so he can continue to learn more about God's Word at Bible College. He has his voice, so he can use it to lift up the name of Jesus and tell others how good He is and that He loves them. He has two hands and arms that work, so he can physically take care of himself. He has his eyes, so he can see God's beautiful creation and praise God with his tongue. He has his ears, so he can hear the 5th grade boys in the Sunday school class he continues to teach. He has great roommates and friends there to help and support him. God is so merciful, even in our valleys.

Matthew 6:25-34 states, "*Therefore I say unto you, Take no thought for your life, what ye shall eat, or what ye shall drink; nor yet for your body, what ye shall put on. Is not the life more than meat, and the body than raiment? Behold the fowls of the air: for they sow not, neither do they reap, nor gather into barns; yet your heavenly Father feedeth them. Are ye not much better than they? Which of you by taking thought can add one cubit unto his stature? And why take ye thought for raiment? Consider the lilies of the field, how they grow; they toil not, neither do they spin: And yet I say unto you, That even Solomon in all his glory was not arrayed like one of these. Wherefore, if God so clothe the grass of the field, which today is, and tomorrow is cast into the oven, shall he not much more clothe you, O ye of little faith? Therefore take no thought, saying, What shall we eat? or, What shall we drink? or, Wherewithal shall we be clothed? For after all these things do the Gentiles seek: for your heavenly Father knoweth that ye have need of all these things. But seek ye first the kingdom of God, and his righteousness; and all these things shall be added unto you. Take therefore no thought for the morrow: for the morrow shall take thought for the things of itself. Sufficient unto the day is the evil thereof.*" In other words, do not worry about or try to control every problem ahead of you. Take it to God in prayer, obey His leading, and trust Him to take care of all your needs and problems. Our lives would be so much easier and stress free if we would learn to allow God to work in our lives instead of becoming anxious, ineffective Christians.

O give thanks unto the LORD, for he is good: for his mercy endureth for ever. Let the redeemed of the LORD say so, whom he hath redeemed from the hand of the enemy; And gathered them out of the lands, from the east, and from the west, from the north, and from the south. They wandered in the wilderness in a solitary way; they found no city to dwell in. Hungry and thirsty, their soul fainted in them. Then they cried unto the LORD in their trouble, and he delivered them out of their distresses. And he led them forth by the right way, that they might go to a city of habitation. Oh that men would praise the LORD for his goodness, and for his wonderful works to the children of men! For he satisfieth the longing soul, and filleth the hungry soul with goodness. Psalm 107:1-9

On Thursday, January 2, 2014, Jacob had ACL total knee auto graft reconstruction surgery. Everything went well and he is able to walk on it. It will take six months of physical therapy, but I know God will help him get back to 100% ability with his knee. After 4 months, Jacob finished his physical therapy ahead of schedule.

Whenever we go through hard times, frustrations, or tragedies, it is so important to learn what God is teaching us through the experience. We should be looking for the blessing He has for us behind the situation and see it as an opportunity for God to bless us instead of a nightmare. God is on our side and desires for us to become more like His Son, Jesus Christ. It is during the valleys in life that we seek and become closer to Him.

We did have some fun with Jacob during his day of surgery and recovery which was in Orlando, Florida. Just for fun, below are listed some quotes from Jacob, his nurse, mom, and dad:

Nurse: "Jacob, do you know where you are?"
Jacob: "California?"
Nurse: "Wow! That is some dream."

Dad: "Jacob, do you want to wear your gown or your shorts home?"
Jacob: "I want to wear my gown to church because they will really like it there."

Jacob: "I want my phone."
After a few minutes and locking himself out of his phone:
Mom: "Do you want me to hold your phone for you? What are you doing?"
Jacob: "I am going to snap chat. No, I want to hold it." He then falls asleep mid-word and drops his phone on the floor.

Nurse: "Do you feel drunk or high?"
Jacob: "I don't know what it feels like to be drunk or high."

Nurse: "Jacob, did you sleep well?"
Jacob: "That was the best sleep I have ever had; can we do that again?"

Nurse: "Try to get Jacob to eat at least a piece of toast today."
Jacob: "I'm starving."
Mom: "Jacob, for lunch, you had a sub sandwich, chips and salsa, and carrots. For dinner, you had Mrs. Carter's roast, potatoes, and carrots."
Jacob: "I'm starving. I want a hamburger and fries."
Mom: "Silly Nurse…"

After we arrived home from the hospital, Jacob and I wait for his dad to come around the van with his crutches:
Jacob: "I can walk."
Mom: "You can't walk today because your leg is numb due to the nerve block. You need to wait and use the crutches."
Jacob: "I can walk, just watch me."
Mom: I talk him out of it as I blocked his exit out of the van. He is one determined, young man.

Jacob claims to not remember any of these conversations.

Lo, children are an heritage of the LORD: and the fruit of the womb is his reward. As arrows are in the hand of a mighty man; so are children of the youth. Happy is the man that hath his quiver full of them: they shall not be ashamed, but they shall speak with the enemies in the gate. Psalm 127:3-5

CHAPTER 36

LEARNING TO LEAN

It is better to trust in the LORD than to put confidence in man. Psalm 118:8

My friends and I have been praying for our college children to get jobs to help pay for their college costs. We are praying fervently for our own and each other's young adults while they are away at college. It seems as if we are being stretched in our faith to trust God to take care of His children and their needs. The more we are stretched, the greater our faith becomes.

I know my God is the Creator and owner of everything, so I know He will take care of me and my children. Seeing God's hands at work in my life and being taken care of by Him in the past assures me I will be taken care of in my future. Faith is a muscle that must be worked out to be increased. God's grace gives you everything you need to accomplish what He has called you to do. If He puts us somewhere or gives us a calling for Him, He will provide us with what is needed at the time it is needed.

We think if we relinquish control of our problems that life will come to an end. In reality, our plans often bring confusion rather than peace. We need to learn that giving up and surrendering it all to God brings our Savior to our rescue. His ways are always so much better than our ways. I never imagine my problem working out the way God leads when I allow Him to take over. His solution is so much greater than I could have even imagined. Backing off and handing the reigns over to God brings peace and a stress-free life. We don't need to worry because we know it is all in God's hands and He always has the best interest of His child in mind. Even when we cannot see the whole picture and it seems like tragedy has occurred, God knows the future and how this hardship will result in lives being blessed later.

We had a full-size truck that was totaled by one of our sons. At the time, it seemed like tragedy and despair. I told myself I was going to look for the blessings instead of being upset and frustrated. It took a lot of work dealing with police, insurance, body shop, etc. In the end when all of the long, irritating hours were over, we had a truck that the insurance company totaled so they gave us money that we used to buy a new car. The new Honda Civic used about half as much gas as the truck. We were blessed through this trial in the end. We need to get into the habit of looking for the blessing and good that comes out of our troubled times.

They that trust in the LORD shall be as mount Zion, which cannot be removed, but abideth for ever. Psalm 125:1

CHAPTER 37

A LONGER JOURNEY

All we like sheep have gone astray; we have turned every one to his own way; and the LORD hath laid on him the iniquity of us all. Isaiah 53:6

Our lives are full of pit stops where it seems all we can do is endure the journey. We cannot escape the situation; we must deal with it until it is finished. Sometimes, we plan and expect these endeavors, and other times they just slap us in the face and dumbfound us. Three trials or undertakings that I have had to face recently are traffic jams, temporary single parenting, and job seeking.

Our son, Caleb, and I were driving home from a two-week visit at my sister's home where he took a SAT Prep class with about twenty other students. Traffic on the interstate was at a standstill; for hours, we inched our way along. This was the most frustrated I have ever been in a traffic situation. We had been traveling for hours and still had hours to go until we would arrive home.

As it turns out, our journey had been prolonged because of a wreck. Hours later, we finally saw the white truck that had been demolished. I thanked God for protecting us from that wreck. We had exited the interstate a few minutes before this to eat lunch at Cracker Barrel. It was not time to serve lunch yet, so we decided to drive until the next restaurant to eat. The time it took us to exit and reenter traffic on I-95, could have placed us in that wreck except for God's divine intervention. We did eventually find another Cracker Barrel restaurant and had a wonderful, tasty, relaxing, and memorable lunch. Caleb took a picture of me that reminds me of the great lunch and time with my son, not the horrific time in traffic just before.

We had planned to be home from our journey at a certain time. Because of the delay, we had a longer journey and arrived home safe and sound but later than expected. No matter how much time you take to plan the details in your life, sometimes you hit unavoidable pot holes which stop you and cause you to look up for help.

My husband, Andy, and our oldest son, Jacob, made a two-week cross country journey driving from our home in Cocoa, Florida to West Coast Baptist College in Lancaster, California. This was an extremely long journey, but a wonderful bonding trip for a father and his son. While dad was gone, I became a temporary single parent. My heart goes out to all single parents who carry this burden alone. You should be honored for your strength and endurance.

My husband is a natural leader. It is a blessing to have him with me as we carry the burdens together. We discuss everything, but he is the final decision maker in our home. While he was gone, we had some work done in our yard. He had already made the decisions of how we would do this and talked with the person he hired. Inevitably, problems arose while he was gone, so I had to contact him and discuss them. He told me to decide what was best since I was home. This was a heavy burden because I did not want to make foolish decisions. My decisions were based on what was most important to us as a couple and to our home.

Wives are not to be the burden bearer or final decision maker, so this was rather heavy for me to carry. I was so relieved when he arrived home and could see with his own eyes and make the final decisions. It is important for husbands to discuss everything with their wives and get their input. Wives think differently than husbands, so another point of view is always helpful. Even if my husband decides against what I suggest, I am pleased that he takes the time to hear me out and get my opinion. He also has to live with whatever decisions he makes because he is responsible before God as the leader of the family.

Seeking God's face in prayer should be an integral part of every decision made. Pray specifically and allow God to lead you. By asking God to go before you, give you wisdom, and take care of the problem, many of our hardships are answered before we have to do anything. Trusting God and allowing Him to work in our lives is so much easier than trying to work it all out on our own.

The third trial I am facing is looking for a job. Our two youngest sons are home schooled seniors this year and are also dual enrolled in the local college; so, my goal is to keep them on target for each class task that needs to be completed each day. Although my tasks as home school teacher are fewer this year, it is still very important that I remain at home and helpful to them in any way needed this final year of high school.

I made a decision to use my spare time this year to write this book. I knew I did not want to go back to work outside the home because I needed our sons to be my primary focus. Since it has been my heart's desire and passion to write this book, I decided this was the perfect time. I also would love to have my book published one day. I would like to become a speaker at ladies conferences and retreats. My goal is to be an encouragement to everyone present.

After I attended a ladies retreat this year, I realized that this dream of speaking would only come to pass if God opens the door for me. God made me realize that He would open the door to His will for my life in ways that I could not even imagine. I decided to keep my hands off of the situation and allow God to work miracles in my life.

I have worked as a Registered Nurse and a teacher in my recent past. I love teaching with a passion. I have taught Science, American Sign Language, and Bible. I also enjoy teaching Speech. Our middle son Tim is taking speech now and I am enjoying giving him instruction and seeing him practice his speeches. I am seeking God's direction and asking Him to open doors so I know to go through them. I am waiting patiently for God to show me the next step to take.

For my thoughts are not your thoughts, neither are your ways my ways, saith the LORD. For as the heavens are higher than the earth, so are my ways higher than your ways, and my thoughts than your thoughts. Isaiah 55:8-9

CHAPTER 38

HOLY, HOLY, HOLY

And they rest not day and night, saying, Holy, holy, holy, Lord God Almighty, which was, and is, and is to come. Revelation 4:8b

The book of Revelation shows us vividly the four angels that are constantly telling God how holy He is. Each of the four angels have a different face: One has the face of a lion, one a calf, one an eagle, and the last one a man. Their job is to constantly say, "Holy, holy, holy" to our Creator God.

As I visualized each face to remember it easier, my mind saw mighty, strong angels whose job is such a blessed one. They are constantly thinking about how holy God is. It brought shame to my soul as I thought about how little I think the same way. I know in my heart how absolutely holy God is, but my thoughts do not stay on that as often as I should.

My heart's desire is to learn to praise God and lift up the name of Jesus continually. It takes unconditional faith to believe that God is the answer to every problem and situation in life. If we are worrying, we do not trust the God who saved our soul from hell with our puny troubles.

Prayer is our way of approaching God specifically with our praise, thanksgiving, and need. As we give God each request about our urgency, we need to stop trying to control and solve the problem ourselves. Allow God to do it for us. Most of us, if not all of us, have issues with control. We feel we must be doing something to deal with our problems instead of waiting on the Lord to come in, rescue us, and be glorified. He is standing there beside us just waiting for our humility and patience. He will not grab the reigns of control from us; we must willingly give them to Him and not grab them back.

Life is so much easier when we allow God to work through us instead of us taking charge and making a mess of everything. If we would learn to give it to God from the very beginning, our lives would be so much less stressful because we completely trust our Savior with every inch of our lives. "Hands off and in God's Hands" is my new life motto. It is hard to get out of the habit of worrying and trying to solve everything by myself, but this motto reminds me to go to God and allow Him to do it His way. As He guides, I need to follow and obey.

When our children are being wronged, I become Mama Bear and want to rush in and roar at whoever is hurting them. I am learning concerning our sons that part of becoming a man is being able to take care of problems on their own. I do my sons an injustice if I teach them that their mom or any woman should be the one rescuing them from their troubles. They will be the men of the house and need to be in charge, not hiding behind a woman's skirt. Our sons are now seventeen, eighteen, and twenty, so they are definitely age appropriate for this task. Pray to God about when you should start this for your own sons. They may be teased mercilessly if they are seen as a mama's boy. This does not mean that mom and dad do not have their back. Of course parents should always be there to support and help them; but not to the point that it keeps them from becoming independent, self-sufficient men. In my devotions today, I memorized Revelation 4:11 which told me about how Holy God is. He is Holy and deserves praise and glory. May my life show forth true praise to God. For He truly is Holy!

Thou are worthy, O Lord, to receive glory and honor and power: For Thou hast created all things, and for thy pleasure they are and were created. Revelation 4:11

CHAPTER 39

ABSENT FROM THE BODY AND PRESENT WITH THE LORD

Precious in the sight of the LORD is the death of his saints. Psalm 116:15

Drying off the tears from my eyes as my friend's funeral just ended, I am reminded of what a powerful impact she had on so many lives. She lived a lifetime of pain, but now is pain free eternally in heaven. As I observed her life, she taught life lessons to many different people no matter their age. She taught foremost to be concerned about other peoples' souls and where they will spend eternity. She was honest and always encouraging to everyone. She told many about Jesus and led them to accept Him as their personal Savior. When she walked, due to health problems, she would waddle. Slowly strolling down the street, she would visit peoples' homes in order to tell them about Jesus and invite them to church.

She was always upbeat and happy even though it was so hard for her to even get out of bed to begin her day. Doing what she could was often a lot more than many well bodied people are willing to ever do. She spent most of her life in a wheelchair or on a scooter. Smiling beautifully, she radiated Jesus Christ and her love for Him and everyone.

She knew how to have fun whether it was driving the singles group around to "toilet paper" a house, or rearranging furniture in a couples' new apartment while they were away. Yes, I was quite surprised to come home to my new, perfectly arranged apartment and find it in shambles. She knew how to have innocent fun. She loved to laugh and knew how to make others laugh along with her.

She had a way of showing love to each and every one that she met by saying encouraging words to uplift you. She knew how to be honest with you in love, guiding you with what was best for you. She played the organ at church and sang like an angel. She was a bossy lady, but we all loved being bossed around by the angel who kept us all in line.

When it is time for your funeral, how will you be remembered? What one word will people use to describe your life on earth? Are you selfish, rude, mean, a liar, untrustworthy? Or, will you be remembered as giving, loving, kind, sweet, caring, and just? The memory of who you were while living should leave a sweet smelling savor and not a stench. The choice of whom you become lies in all the decisions you make in your life. Choose wisely.

Blessed are they that keep his testimonies, and that seek him with the whole heart. Psalm 119:2

CHAPTER 40

WHAT ARE YOU CHASING?

The steps of a good man are ordered by the LORD: and he delighteth in his way.
Psalm 37:23

I woke up from such a vivid dream that I wanted to go back to sleep and finish it to see how it would end. Unfortunately I could not fall back asleep, so I concentrated on every detail and visualized it descriptively in my mind. I usually forget my dreams almost immediately, so I knew I would have to really concentrate to remember.

It begins with my husband and me driving along an old, dirt road. We are driving toward a bridge spanning a roaring river below. All of a sudden Andy speeds up to be able to jump the area between the dirt road and land on the wooden bridge. This chocolate colored bridge was unlike any I had seen before. It only had two wooden slats which would support the car wheels as you drive across.

The problem with our speeding up was that there was a bus in front of us already on the bridge. In order to avoid hitting the bus that had stopped, Andy turned a hard left and to my absolute dread sent our vehicle into the river below. Time seemed to stop as we were midair and all I could think was, "I cannot believe this is really happening." The jeep we were in impacted the water with a jolt that made my bones ache.

The next thing I remember is swimming to the side of the river and crawling onto the river bank. I see that Andy is in the jeep and driving it backwards out of the river to get back in line for the bridge again. I start walking up the sandy hill to the road beside the bridge so I can get back into the jeep with him. As I am walking up, several teens grab blue bikes that are used to ride across the bridge. I guess no walking across the bridge is allowed. I look right and don't see Andy or the jeep, so I look left toward the bridge. I see a left hand stuck out of the window and flagging me down, thinking it is Andy. I then notice the hand is covered in a plastic see through glove. This tells me it is not Andy. I stand there dumb founded as I search for my husband who has apparently disappeared into thin air. The line of vehicles and blue bicycles grows longer behind the bridge as people anxiously prepare to cross. I am left there alone, not knowing what to do.

In life, we can become so much a part of the crowd that subsequently all we become are followers. As Christians, we should stand out and stand-alone if necessary to do what God calls us to do. Are you chasing the latest fad, electronic game, or newest iPhone? God has more for us to accomplish in life besides becoming a number, a gamer, or a tech geek. There is nothing wrong with dressing nicely, playing games, or even having the newest technical device as long as it does not control our lives to the point of making us unusable for the glory of God.

Sometimes we get involved in ministries or work because our friends are doing it instead of asking God how we can be used best for His glory. God has a path that is best for us if we are willing to surrender to His will and way and trust His guidance. Many people fear failure so much that they do not even attempt what God lays on their hearts. Failure may come, but that should not defeat us. We need to learn from our failures and mistakes and become better because of them.

Perhaps life becomes a routine of working, eating, and sleeping day in and out. We feel like a hamster on a hamster wheel getting nowhere. This is a time to do some introspection and prayer as to where God would have you be the best for Him. Don't stay comfortable where you are if God is leading you elsewhere.

People who do much for the glory of God are the ones who are willing to dream big and follow God even if it scares them to take the next step. They have worked hard and prepared to do what is ahead of them. They have prayed and fasted to know God's perfect will for their lives. They do not allow fear to stop them from proceeding with their work and ministry. Courage is not being without fear, it is setting fear aside while you proceed on. Whatever happens to a Christian, he or she is never alone because the Holy Spirit never leaves nor forsakes.

God does not promise an easy road, but He does promise to go each step of the way with us. The best and safest place to be is in God's will. It is best because we are bringing God glory and giving others the gospel. It is safest because when it is time for you to die; you will die, no matter where you are. If it is not God's timing for you to die, you will not die. It is wise to pray daily for God's hedge of protection over you; to keep evil away from you; and that you would have boldness to do what God asks you to do every day.

If God is asking you to do something, you need to immediately submit and surrender to His will. You will be unhappy and not content out of His will. Seek God's face with prayer and fasting before you make decisions. Relinquish all pride as you seek His guidance in your life. His ways are always better than our ways. He can see the whole picture of our lives from start to finish. He knows everything and has all wisdom. Why do we trust our Savior with our salvation, but not with our lives? He is the great creator of all things and wants His best for our lives. We need to learn to surrender all of ourselves to Him wholeheartedly and then watch His hand work in our lives. We need to take our hands off and put everything in God's hands. He already knows what the embroidery front side looks like when all we see is the chaotic, jumbled mess on the back side. Trust in Him who knows all and sees all.

Today a decision will be made at the crossroads. Which way will I turn? Do I choose the enticing pleasure of sin for a season, or do I choose the straight and narrow way of following God's will and His best for my life? Do I sow selfishness, pride, and covetousness? Or do I sow in others, humility, and contentment? As a Christian, I will face pitfalls and traps every day that will affect the rest of my life. Pregnancy, AIDS, drunk driving, manslaughter, jail, and evil thoughts are only a few consequences for sins I may choose. Or do I choose abstinence until marriage, virginity, saying "NO!" to drugs, alcohol, and pornography?

Allowing the Holy Spirit to control our actions instead of lustful desires is a constant choice all Christians must make. Looking ahead to possible temptations and finding ways to avoid the pitfalls is a daily plan that many do not see as necessary. I take careful, thoughtful steps instead of running ahead and constantly stepping on mines that explode in my face. Why is it that we take more time to study how to beat a video game than we take to be aware of and to avoid sin traps in our lives?

PLAN:
   Pray for God to put a hedge of protection about us daily.
   Learn verses against sins that we have trouble with.
   Accountability every day with someone we trust with our failures
   New mercies every morning

"The two biggest little words in the English language are the two little words, do right..." -Bob Jones, Sr.

Be still, and know that I am God. Psalm 46:10a

CHAPTER 41

HELL IS FULL OF RELIGIOUS PEOPLE

And in hell he lift up his eyes, being in torments, and seeth Abraham afar off, and Lazarus in his bosom. Luke 16:23

Hell is full of religious people who are probably confused as to why they are there. Salvation does not come from good works, who your parents are, or even attending church faithfully. It is so simple that even a small child can understand, but salvation is continuously rejected by so many.

Looking up from the depths of hell, she screams while being tormented in her flame. She is haunted by the memory again and again: She is walking gingerly because of her age. She and her Yorkshire dog are enjoying the light breeze on this cool, fall morning. She looks ahead and sees a young lady walking briskly down the sidewalk. The young lady waves a happy "hello" with a smile; then she continues on ahead.

She looks ahead to the end of the sidewalk and sees the young lady turn around and starts strolling back in her direction. As she approaches, the young lady takes off her sunglasses, pulls her earphones out of her ears, stops beside her, and hands her a gospel tract. She is being invited to a local church.

She thanks the young lady and tells her that she really does not go to church. She is married to a man who is religious also and she believes in whatever god or Jesus there is, so she feels good about herself. She is asked if she is trusting in her good works to get herself to heaven. She says she is. She is asked to take a good person test where she is shown that because of the lies she has told and other sins she has committed, she is not perfect and cannot get to heaven on her own merits.

She remembers as the young lady continues to give Bible verse after verse to show how she cannot get to heaven on her own. Romans 3:23 states, *"For all have sinned and come short of the glory of God."* Romans 6:23 says, *"For the wages of sin is death, but the gift of God is eternal life through Jesus Christ our Lord."* She has never memorized these verses, but from hearing the young lady quote them to her, they are eternally branded into her memory.

Why did she interrupt the young lady and not allow her to continue? Why did she think she was good enough even though deep inside she knew she was full of sin? Why did she not fall to her knees and beg forgiveness and ask Jesus for salvation? Why? Why? Why?

She made some small talk and never allowed the conversation to go back to Jesus again. As she walked away from the young lady, in her mind she knew she was not perfect. What difference does it make? If there really is a God, wouldn't He be loving and kind and forgive her if she is not good enough? She must have covered all of the bases religiously. She doesn't ever condemn anyone. Everyone can believe any way they want to and still be Ok, right?

As she walked on into the last days of her short life on earth, she tried to find solace in her empty life. Her children and grandchildren have now moved away. She has her dog that gives her companionship and great joy. She thinks to herself, "Isn't there more to life than this?"

The young lady walks away saddened in her heart knowing that this woman is rejecting Jesus as her Savior and on her way to hell. "If only I could make her see and believe; but it is her choice." She prays and asks God to open the lady's eyes to see her need for Jesus as Savior. She asks the Holy Spirit to give her boldness to continue to tell others about Jesus and that many will come to know Him before it is too late.

Looking back over the years of my life, I was thinking of so many people that I have told about Jesus who have rejected Him as Savior. I know they are on the fast track to hell and my heart is saddened. My job is to tell; the Holy Spirit's job is to convict and save from hell. Together, we can win many souls as long as I do my part. The Holy Spirit is always bold and does His job. May I always be filled with the Holy Spirit so He can work in and through me to bring others to Jesus as their Savior.

And he said unto them, Go ye into all the world, and preach the gospel to every creature. Mark 16:15

CHAPTER 42

MAILBOX SURPRISE

Give, and it shall be given unto you; good measure, pressed down, and shaken together, and running over, shall men give into your bosom. For with the same measure that ye mete withal it shall be measured to you again. Luke 6:38

Opening my mailbox door each day brings a tad bit of excitement that is like walking into the living room on Christmas morning and anxiously waiting to open the wrapped gifts. I look inside the mailbox and see a small package. I pull it out and excitedly look at the return address. I also see that it is addressed to me and my husband.

The package has a sealed and taped envelope inside and it feels thick. I decide to wait until my husband gets back from the library for us to open it together. I call him to see how long it will be before he arrives home. Minutes later, he pulls into the driveway. I bring the envelope to him and wait impatiently like a child on Christmas morning holding a gift in her hands. Finally, he stops what he is doing and watches me as I open the envelope.

Peeling back the tape off of both sides, I tear into the top of the envelope. I reach inside to see a hand written note and gift wrap paper. I open it to find five gift cards. I yell with excitement and jump up and down. My husband looks at me like I just went a little crazy and then asks, "Well, what is it?" I tell him as I spread out God's blessings before us. We are both so happy and blessed. I read the note that was included. It says, "This is sent with God's blessings; when you use it, thank the Lord, for it comes from Him. He just used us as a channel of blessing at this time.

Our Lord knows the way through the wilderness, all you have to do is follow Him. "

This love gift was sent to us while my husband was on furlough from his job. This truly was a gift directly from God. I had been praying specifically for certain needs and they were answered. God likes to see us get excited about how and when He blesses us. He likes us to thank Him and not take Him for granted. With the Wal-Mart and Visa Gift cards, we will be able to buy the items we will need. We also were sent a Chick-fil-A gift card. My husband and I were able to go on a lunch date because of this blessing from others.

Gas is expensive, but it is a necessity to get to all of the places we need to go. I had been praying specifically for gas cards or money for gas. I love how God answers specific prayer requests. Something I am learning through this furlough experience is to ask those without jobs or going through hard times specifically what their needs are. If someone would come up to me and ask me what we need, I would tell them. God has laid it on my heart not to go to people or the church to ask for things, but that He would supply our needs His own way. His ways are so much better than anything we could imagine, so I choose to rely upon Him and to continue to pray for specific needs. I am also discovering that He will supply your needs right when you need them, not before. He wants your full dependence to be upon Him and wants you to seek Him daily.

Looking forward to the day when this furlough experience is over for us, I want to take what I have learned and apply it to helping others with their specific needs. You don't ask, "How are you doing, are you OK?" You should ask, "What is a specific need that I can help supply you with today?" I would be rejoicing over someone giving us mustard, toilet paper, or Tide. You don't have to give a lot; everyone has something they can give to others to be a blessing.

After my husband returned to work, we asked our Singles Sunday School class to help with this year's Christmas giving project by signing up to bring five items on a list to give to five families in our church who are unemployed or going through hard times financially. Everyone participated and gave with joy. God allows us to experience hard times in our lives so we will be empathetic to others going through the same situations. We bagged up all of the items for the five families. As we delivered the items and saw the happiness it brought to each one, our hearts were filled with joy knowing personally how much each item was appreciated.

Every man according as he purposeth in his heart, so let him give; not grudgingly, or of necessity: for God loveth a cheerful giver. 2 Corinthians 9:7

CHAPTER 43

UNCLEAN SPIRITS TRYING TO TRIP ME UP

Wherefore let him that thinketh he standeth take heed lest he fall.
1 Corinthians 10:12

Today in church, the preacher spoke about how unclean spirits try to trip you up by whispering negative or bad thoughts in your ear. As Christians, we are fully possessed by the Holy Spirit, so demons cannot possess us; but they can oppress or bother us and try to influence us. I completely understood what was being talked about, because I am constantly fighting with unclean spirits trying to make me give up or to not care about being an effective Christian for Jesus Christ.

Once saved, Satan and unclean spirits know they cannot get our soul, so they work their hardest to keep us from telling others about Jesus and being useful Christians. Unclean spirits are around us enough to know what tactic works best to hinder each of us. They are excellent liars. For some, it may be discouragement and feeling unloved. Others may be distracted with pleasurable activities such as fishing, hunting, or some other activity will keep them away from church and becoming closer to our Savior.

For me personally, it is worry. I grew up in a Christian family that went to church regularly. I have heard about God's Word and all of the true Bible stories it contains. When I was ten, my daddy became sick with cancer; two years later, he was in heaven. He left behind a widow who had an eighth grade education, a sixteen year old daughter, a seven year old son, and me, a twelve year old daughter. These times of being a teenager without a father and seeing a widowed mother take care of her three children taught me to trust God.

As had occurred many times before, my mom and I went grocery shopping together at a store a couple of miles from our home. We were in the checkout with all of our groceries ready to pay when my mom turns to me and asks me to go walk away for a few minutes. I was at the age to find this a little strange, so I turn back to look as I am walking away and I see my mom pulling food stamps out of a book. I was old enough to know what they were and what it meant. To me, it meant that we did not have enough money to even buy food. I was not embarrassed. I was glad my mom was doing whatever it took to feed her family. I did, however, grow up a lot at that moment in my life. Perhaps this was the starting place of worry for me.

Through the next few years as I lived at home prior to leaving for college, my faith actually grew. I would see our needs being met. We were never without food and when we needed clothing, God provided. I often wonder how we were able to attend a Christian school. My mom made that a first priority and likely, we were on a scholarship of some kind. Instead of worrying, I just trusted God to provide and was content with what I had.

When people live through tough times, many want to make those times just go away; it is through these times that we grow spiritually by gaining faith and learning to trust God. I grew up having to trust God because there was no other option. When I am going through a tough time, like I am at this very moment with my husband being furloughed and not having any pay coming in from his job, my first thought would be to make this hurry up and end. No one likes being out of their comfort zone. I have decided to trust God throughout this ordeal and I want to learn as much as I can so I can be a help to others when this part of our lives is completed.

My mom did get her GED later in life after I left for college. I am so proud of her for that. She had to care for my little brother, James, who is a slow learner. One thing that really impressed me about my mom in addition to her absolute strength to carry on was her desire to help my little brother become all that he could. She would take him weekly to the University of Florida for them to work with him. He did graduate from high school with a special diploma. He recently was awarded with the great honor of Volunteer of the Year by the county where he lives. He has volunteered at a Senior Citizen Center for fifteen years and everyone loves him there. My sister, brother, mother, and I were blessed to be able to spend a week together this past summer. My mom had an aneurysm burst in her brain in 1991. Today she has many hardships she deals with due to that brain trauma. My Aunt Nancy is an angel who takes care of her and my brother. It was such a wonderful week for all four of us to be together. My brother is 43 years old now and has become a wonderful, caring man of whom I am very proud.

If I allow myself to dwell on all of the bills piling up, the surgery my son needs in December, the gas we need, the food we need, the laundry detergent, toilet paper, electricity and water, my mind can be influenced by the unclean spirits who are wanting so much to deflate my faith. My faith has grown greatly though my life and I know my God will take care of me. My oldest son told me the other day that he is amazed with how great my faith is. I know this made the unclean spirits angry, giving them a new challenge. I am constantly reminded that the Lord will help me. I do not need to fear.

As Christians, we must be on the lookout for unclean spirits who are trying to influence us. We must recognize their voices immediately and defy them with truth from the Word of God. They are liars and are seeking to make us accept their constant lies. We must quote verses out loud with confidence so they will hear them also. They cannot read our minds. If we deny these lies with God's Word, eventually the unclean spirits cannot do anything to us at that moment and will leave us alone. We must be on the constant lookout because they like to surprise us and knock us to our knees if we are not ready at all times. Some of my favorite verses are I Peter 5:7-8, *"Casting all your care upon Him, for He careth for you. Be sober, be vigilant, because your adversary, the devil, as a roaring lion, walketh about, seeking whom He may devour."* These verses tell us how to defeat unclean spirits. We must first cast our negative thoughts or worries onto the Lord knowing that He cares for us. Then, we must be on watch and guard against unclean spirits lying to us. We must know in our hearts that we are soldiers in God's army and the enemy is constantly trying to kill our potency for the kingdom of God. We must also be prepared with the armor of God which is the helmet of salvation, the chest plate of righteousness, the loins of truth, our feet shod with the preparation of the gospel of peace, the shield of faith which defeats all the darts of the wicked, and the Sword of the Spirit, which is the Word of God. We must pray for wisdom and seek God's face daily. We must never allow pride to lead us because it guarantees a fall. We must be looking for the pitfalls that we usually fall into and avoid them. I have learned to stop listening to or reading about the news of the furlough because the unclean spirits will shoot darts about it at me all day long. I know that God will take care of this situation in His timing and that my job is to remain faithful, on guard, and learning from everything I face each day.

One of the best ways to stop worrying about your own problems is to seek ways to encourage others. I like to ask the Lord to tell me someone who needs something from me today and what I can do or send to them to encourage them. I like to send cards or small gifts to those who need encouraging. Just now, God laid a friend on my mind and what exactly I should give her. Even if we are in need, we always have something we can give, even if it is just a smile and a kind word.

There hath no temptation taken you but such as is common to man: but God is faithful, who will not suffer you to be tempted above that ye are able; but will with the temptation also make a way to escape, that ye may be able to bear it. 1 Corinthians 10:13

CHAPTER 44

CRYING OUT TO JESUS

And who knoweth whether thou art come to the kingdom for such a time as this?
Esther 4:14b

Facing the possibility of the total genocide of her people, Esther stood tall and strong risking her own death. In the end, the king declared that the Jews could defend themselves on the day that it was legal to kill all Jews and take their possessions. The Jews survived and it became a day of feasting and celebration because God had protected them. When we face tragedy in our lives, we need to look to God to take the chaos and turn it into a day of celebrating and feasting. We need to ask, "God, how may I give you glory in this hard time?" Instead of crawling into a corner and crying, we should put on our Armor of God and be ready to fight against the darts of the devil. (Ephesians 6:11-18) Stand tall Christians.

Have you ever been in a situation where the only thing you can do is cry out to Jesus for help? This morning on my typical bike ride I was pedaling along when all of a sudden beside me on the right side was a pit bulldog running with me. Before I could process what was happening, another pit bulldog was on the left side of me also running along. The usual response would be to freak out, but I had just prayed the Armor of God which surrounded me with peace.

They started to run in front of me and then finally one of the dogs stopped. I slam on my brakes and head off the sidewalk into the grass. Then the dogs come beside me. One jumps on my leg and arm. I realized later how powerfully intense it hit me as my arm and leg were bruised and tender. A Good Samaritan or angel stopped her car and honked the horn to get the dogs' attention. While they run to the car, I start to ride off again. Of course they follow me. I know this next part is not logical, but I decide to try to outrun them. Of course that doesn't work. They start to go in front of me again. I know where that leads, so I pedal off of the sidewalk and am about to cross traffic on the side street. The last car is crossing so I can't safely proceed until the driver of the car slows down. I go behind the car with the dogs following. Traffic on the main street is stopped at the red light. There are about five or six vehicles all watching me and the dogs. I see the third vehicle has the windows down, so I yell at them telling them these dogs won't stop following me. They honk their horn to distract the dogs and I pedal ahead. Soon I see another angel or Good Samaritan riding his bike towards me. He gives me a look that says he will take care of the dogs and everything is Ok. I keep looking and moving forward and do not look back because I know I am safe and secure in the arms of God.

The fear of man bringeth a snare: but whoso putteth his trust in the LORD shall be safe. Proverbs 29:25

CHAPTER 45

GIVE GOD YOUR SCRAPBOOK LIFE PAGE

Remember the days of old, consider the years of many generations: ask thy father, and he will shew thee; thy elders, and they will tell thee. Deuteronomy 32:7

As high school graduates, most, if not all of us, have kept some special keepsake to invoke memories of days gone by. Perhaps, you have a scrapbook full of memories. As I awoke this morning, I was thinking about how our two youngest sons, Timothy and Caleb, will be graduating from high school this May. I have a scrapbook that I plan to give to each of them today so they can begin collecting and creating their own memories.

God reminded me how it is so much easier in life if we give Him our scrapbook page of life and allow Him to put the right pieces and people where they should go. He knows all and it is like a genius helping a two-year old. But, like most two-year olds, we have a little temper tantrum and want to do it our own way. We spend hours upon hours to place pieces on our page and glue them messily around, thinking we are doing a great job. At the end of the day when we look at our completed page, we see the reality of the mess we have made. We then look to Jesus and ask Him to help us. He tells us He has been patiently waiting for us to ask Him. He lovingly and carefully removes the mess and gunk. He wipes it clean and starts over. This is painful for us because of all the time and useless effort we have put forth. Jesus begins again and this time He chooses each picture, art piece, and word. He applies them in the best places on our life's page.

As we watch Him work, we are amazed because we never would have thought to do it that way. When He finishes His masterpiece and shows us His finished work, we look upon the page with awe. "Wow, I never would have thought my life could have accomplished that." Jesus smiles at us and quietly turns the page as we lie down in our warm, comfy beds and fall asleep. We rest and awake the next morning ready to start our new page of life. Today, will we forget and start yesterday's process all over again, or will we remember to trust Jesus because He knows what is best for our lives? Trusting Jesus and seeking Him is so much easier than the daily chaos we make out of our lives. Allow Him to work on your scrapbook page of life today and every day.

Being confident of this very thing, that He which hath begun a good work in you will perform it until the day of Jesus Christ. Philippians 1:6

NOTES

Chapter One

1. Koyczan, Shane, "To This Day Project". YouTube. Web. 19 Feb. 2013.

Chapter Two

2. "Timeline of Events in the Boston Marathon Bombing". ABC News.com. Web.
12 April 2014.

3. "Three People Killed, Hundreds Injured in Boston Marathon Bombing". 2014. The History Channel Website.
http://www.history.com/this-day-in-history/three-people-killed-hundreds-injured-in-Boston-Marathon-bombing. Web. 15 April 2013.

4. "108 Hours: Inside the Hunt for the Boston Marathon Bombers". 2014. NBC News.com. Boston Bombing Anniversary: 75 Stories. Web. 15 April 2014.

Chapter Four

5. Maxwell, John. The Five Levels of Leadership. London: Hodder & Stoughton Ltd., 2011. Print.

Chapter Seventeen

6. Reber, Paul. "What is the Memory Capacity of the Human Brain?" Scientific American Mind. April 2010. Print.

ABOUT THE AUTHOR

Sandra L. Bundy is a wife of 27 years and a mother of three grown sons. She is a registered nurse, but her true passions are teaching and writing. She taught junior high and high school students American Sign Language, science, and Bible. She was also a home school teacher for her sons over the course of five years through their high school graduations. Her encouragement ministry goals are to show the love of Jesus to others, to encourage others toward daily spiritual growth, and to give encouragement through personal life experiences. She intends to continue writing, publishing books, and pursuing speaking opportunities at ladies retreats and meetings worldwide.